DR. MYLES MUNROE

FOREWORD BY JOHN MAXWELL

THE

FATHERHOOD
PRINCIPLE

PRIORITY, POSITION, AND THE ROLE OF THE MALE

WHITAKER
HOUSE

THE FATHERHOOD PRINCIPLE:
Priority, Position, and the Role of the Male
(Revised and Expanded Hardcover Edition of *The Principle of Fatherhood*)

Dr. Myles Munroe
Bahamas Faith Ministries International
P.O. Box N9583
Nassau, Bahamas
e-mail: bfmadmin@bfmmm.com
websites: www.bfmmm.com; www.bfmi.tv; www.mylesmunroe.tv

ISBN: 978-1-60374-026-5
Printed in the United States of America
© 2000, 2008 by Dr. Myles Munroe

Whitaker House
1030 Hunt Valley Circle
New Kensington, PA 15068
www.whitakerhouse.com

Library of Congress Cataloging-in-Publication Data
Munroe, Myles.
The fatherhood principle : priority, position, and the role of the male / Myles
Munroe. — Hardcover ed.
p. cm.
ISBN 978-1-60374-026-5 (trade hardcover : alk. paper) 1. Fatherhood—Religious
aspects—Christianity. I. Title.
BV4529.17.M86 2008
248.8'421—dc22
2008004765

1 2 3 4 5 6 7 8 9 10 11 12 **Ⱳ** 16 15 14 13 12 11 10 09 08

Dedication

To all men everywhere, especially in Third World nations, who desire to return to the original blueprint of true fatherhood.

To my Dad, my beloved father, the Reverend Matthias E. Munroe, the greatest role model of fatherhood in my life—a distinguished man of character, strength, loyalty, commitment, love for my mother, and successful sustainer of eleven grateful and grace-filled children. Thank you, Dad, for living the lessons of life that formed the foundation of the principles in this book.

To my late beloved brother, Paul, who became my twin in life and showed me how to love God without compromise. I know you are now with the Father of fathers.

To my father-in-law, Captain Halton Lockhart, who fathered the woman who has become the wife of my life. Thank you for your steady love and support and for being my other father.

To my beloved son, Chario (Myles, Jr.), who makes me live up to the fatherhood image of God. May your sons also become true fathers in their generation.

To my brothers, Oscar and Garth, may you continue to be models of the Father's love for your wives and children.

To all the members of the Bahamas Faith Ministries Fellowship Real Men Ministry. Thank you for allowing me to teach and develop these principles through your submission to the ministry.

To the born and unborn sons of men who neglected to show them how to be fathers. May this book help father you to become better fathers to your sons.

ACKNOWLEDGMENTS

Everything we accomplish in life is a synergistic product of many people who have contributed to what we have done and who we have become. This work is no different. I am eternally grateful to all the great men who have inspired, encouraged, and corrected me throughout my development over the years. It takes true fathers to produce true fathers.

I want to thank the following people for their contribution to the development and completion of this work:

Dad, for laying the foundation for my life so that this book could be not just a theory, but a result of my living the principles you taught and lived before me all my life.

My beloved wife, Ruth, and my precious children, Charisa and Chairo (Myles, Jr.), whose births made me a father and placed demands on me to exemplify the principles of true fatherhood. Thank you for all your patience with me as I developed as a husband and a father.

The many spiritual fathers in my life whose lives and character further refined mine: Dr. Oral Roberts; the late Dr. Tunel Nelson; Dr. Ezekiel Guti; Rev. Bob Stamps; Rev. Duke Smith; the late Dr. H. W. Brown; my oldest brother, Oscar Munroe; my late brother, Paul Munroe; and my youngest brother, Garth Munroe; my brothers-in-law, Henry Francis, Jose Johnson, Steve Hall, and Richard Pinder; and my father-in-law, Captain Halton Lockhart.

Finally, to the Father of our Lord Jesus Christ, the Creator and Sustainer of all things, the ultimate Father of fathers, Elohim.

Contents

FOREWORD

B eing a father is the most fulfilling job a man can have. As Christian parents, we have the unique opportunity to make an eternal investment in the lives of our children.

Jesus often referred to God as "Father." God the Father gives unconditional love, leadership, and guidance. He protects and allows us to learn by His words. God has entrusted us with His sacred title: Father.

In the last few decades, society has strayed away from the importance that fatherhood holds. We have seen the family redefined so much that, in many cases, the father is not even present. The traditional family is fading away, and, with it, we are losing God's blessing and missing the mark.

Becoming a good father is not automatic—it takes time and effort. We must be willing to invest in this job—our most important, second to being a husband—as any other career we might pursue. A father should present the fundamental qualities of leadership, responsibility, and accountability, as well as the capabilities of planning, disciplining, and loving. Fathering is a full-time job. As men, we must train, develop, and learn to be that which God intended for our families.

In his book, *The Fatherhood Principle*, Dr. Myles Munroe provides a fresh look at time-tested principles for men to measure their effectiveness as fathers in our modern society.

Dr. Munroe teaches how the role, vision, relationship, management, and communication skills of the father within the family structure apply to societies everywhere and at all levels. His fatherhood tips in each chapter challenge me to apply their principles.

In a time when there are classes, books, and workshops for every skill and hobby, I would challenge every father to take time to invest in his most important role—fatherhood. A good father is priceless, as are the children they lead and invest in. We need more good fathers, and this book is an invaluable tool that will indeed help meet that need.

—Dr. John C. Maxwell
Author and Speaker
Founder, The INJOY Group

PREFACE

"D
ad is destiny." The words sprang from the page in *U.S. News & World Report*[1] and exploded in my mind like an atom bomb. I could not believe what I was reading. Even more surprising was the source of those words— seemingly taken right from the heart of one of my old seminar sessions. For over twenty-five years, I have lectured, taught, and counseled thousands of individuals on the subjects of relationships, family development, and marriage. One of the greatest concerns I have carried over these years is the male crisis facing most of our communities. I have repeatedly stated and emphatically declared that the key to the restoration and preservation of a sane and healthy society is the salvaging of the male, especially as a responsible father. But to find those words on the pages of one of our most popular news magazines was cause for great encouragement and excitement.

I am a trainer in human and leadership development and founded one of the most dynamic churches in Nassau, Bahamas. Therefore, it was a source of enormous comfort and relief to see that contemporary behavioral scientists, psychologists, and government bodies were finally agreeing on a conclusion that many of us who deal with social and spiritual matters have known all along.

The statement "Dad is destiny" embodies both the problem and the solution for the majority of our societies' ills. In it

---

[1] Joseph P. Shapiro, Joannie M. Schrof, Mike Tharp, and Dorian Friedman, "Honor Thy Children," *U.S.News & World Report*, February 27, 1995.

lies the key to the salvation and restoration of mankind. About twenty-five hundred years ago, the biblical prophet Malachi spoke of the work and purpose of the coming Messiah by declaring, *"He will turn the hearts of the fathers to their children, and the hearts of the children to their fathers"* (Malachi 4:6). The implication is that the divine assessment of man's fundamental problem is that it is a fatherless problem.

U.S.News & World Report stated that "more than virtually any other factor, a biological father's presence in the family will determine a child's success and happiness." Without a doubt, this secular article read like a Sunday morning sermon taken from the books of the Bible. It was a refreshing reminder that no matter how far we as a society may stray, it is impossible to effectively ignore, deny, or improve on the ancient wisdom and fundamental truth and principles embedded in the biblical records. The Bible establishes in its very first chapters the critical and pivotal role of the male, as well as his fatherhood responsibility.

Let's take a brief reality check on the status of our modern-day society and its impact on this and future generations:

> Rich or poor, white or black, the children of divorce and those born outside marriage struggle through life at a measurable disadvantage, according to a growing chorus of social thinkers....
>
> [Many social scientists and behavioral experts] challenge the view that external forces like street crime, lousy schools and economic stress lie behind the crisis in families. The revised thinking is that it's the breakdown in families that feeds social ills.[2]

---

[2] Ibid.

The National Fatherhood Initiative compiles information from a variety of sources on the effects of fatherlessness on many social problems, including poverty, maternal and child health, incarceration, crime, teen pregnancy, child abuse, drug and alcohol abuse, education, and childhood obesity. Here is some of the disturbing data they have collected:

- Children in father-absent homes are five times more likely to be poor.
- Infant mortality rates are 1.8 times higher for infants of unmarried mothers than for married mothers.
- Youths in father-absent households still had significantly higher odds of incarceration than those in mother-father families.
- Youths are more at risk of first substance use without a highly involved father.
- Being raised by a single mother raises the risk of teen pregnancy.
- Fatherless children are twice as likely to drop out of school.
- Compared to living with both parents, living in a single-parent home doubles the risk that a child will suffer physical, emotional, or educational neglect.[3]

An absent father can have an effect on a person's economic prospects beyond childhood. According to a report by the U.S. Department of Labor, today's fatherlessness

> ...may bode ill for tomorrow's labor force, at least if the predictions of economic theory are correct. In

---

[3] https://www.fatherhood.org/father_factor.asp, February 6, 2008.

Becker's (1981) model, for example, children raised in families with fewer resources tend to have lower human capital. Thus economic theory would predict that, all else equal, the next generation of workers will enter the labor market with less human capital than the last. [4]

Research has shown that even individuals who survive the trauma and negative impact of a broken home or marriage still suffer socio-psychological maladjustments. The emotional, psychological, spiritual, and moral needs met by the loving, caring, balanced environment of a strong marriage and family unit cannot be substituted.

It is understandable that there are no perfect human specimens in the human race; however, social sciences have concluded that when an individual is incubated within an atmosphere of love, unity, and caring between two parental elements, there is a definite transfer of those qualities and characteristics to the next generation. In essence, the human family produces after its own kind. The natural, logical process of reproduction, which involves the intimate consummation of two individuals, gives evidence that the Creator designed the human family to procreate within the context of a strong, stable union structured to provide the social, psychological, emotional, physical, and spiritual environment for successful development.

There is further evidence that there are critical emotional and psychological needs that only a male can provide, just as

[4] Jeff Grogger and Nick Ronan, "The Intergenerational Effects of Fatherlessness on Educational Attainment and Entry-Level Wages," September 1995, Bureau of Labor Statistics, U.S. Department of Labor, http://www.bls.gov/ore/abstract/nl/nl950080.htm, February 6, 2008.

there are specific needs only the female is designed to meet. Therefore, the absence of either has an effect on development, despite the seemingly normal functioning of the human family.

The negative statistics of fatherlessness can be reversed by the power of fathers restored to their place in the family and their true calling as men. We can reverse these downward trends and strengthen lives, families, communities, and nations by discovering and living out the priority, position, and role of the male in the family.

—Dr. Myles Munroe

Introduction

The greatest enemy of man is ignorance of self. Nothing is more frustrating than not knowing who you are or what to do with what you have. It is debilitating to have something but not know what it is for or how to use it. Even more frustrating is to have an assignment but not know how to fulfill it. Ever had that problem? As a student, did you ever take home an assignment and not know how to complete it but still try your best to do it all by yourself? Remember that feeling of sitting up all night, trying hard, failing, and finally getting angry with everyone, including yourself? How terrible it is to be given something to do but not possess the understanding of how to do it. This is a cause of greatest distress.

We Lack Understanding of Ourselves

All of mankind's problems are a result of one major dilemma. What's this dilemma? Possession without comprehension; assignment without instruction; resources without knowledge; having everything but not knowing why. Essentially, the dilemma is that we lack understanding. Without understanding, life is an experiment, and frustration is the reward.

I'll never forget bringing home my algebra homework from junior high school in the Bahamas, where I've lived all my life. Have you ever taken algebra? Remember all those formulas? For me, it was the most difficult subject in school.

Some students had an aptitude for math, particularly algebra, geometry, or calculus. I didn't. Learning algebra was a horrible experience for me.

Understanding those many formulas was my problem. I remember getting homework assignments consisting of six problems to solve per page. I would go home and just sit there staring at those things. No matter what I did, since I did not understand the formulas, I could not solve the problems.

I would become frustrated to the point of tears. I knew I would get punished in the morning if I didn't understand the formulas and come up with the correct answers. What did I do? I faked it! I wrote down whatever figures came to my mind. Having some numbers written on the page may have looked good, so I thought, but all the answers were incorrect.

This is more than just an interesting story. You see, when it comes to the issues of life, we often do the same thing I did with my algebra assignments. When problems arise, we don't understand the problems, much less life itself, so we fake it. Although I tried to make the figures work out the way I wanted, they were wrong because I didn't understand the formulas. When test time came, my lack of understanding brought me the final result of faking it—failure.

One day I decided I had better learn and understand those formulas, so I took a tutoring course after school with my teacher. I put forth the time and effort, and even though it took me hours, one by one, I began to understand the formulas! Every time I understood them, a lightbulb went off in my mind. Algebra finally made sense to me and eventually became easy. The fear I had was now replaced with confidence.

After I began understanding algebra, I took home my assignments with a smile. Before understanding algebra, I went home with fear. By overcoming my lack of understanding, I was able to approach those problems with confidence.

The minute you understand and learn the principles of how to do something, then no matter what figures are given to you, you'll just plug them into the proper formula. The figures can change any number of ways, but the formula remains the same. Understanding how to use the formula and how to plug the numbers in correctly gives you the right answer.

> **You need to learn the purpose, principles, and functions of true fatherhood.**

Principles are very much like formulas. They are set laws that govern life and are constant in the face of change. The key, then, is learning and understanding the principles so you can handle any configuration, any problem, or any situation in life. When you understand the principles of life, it doesn't matter what life throws at you—just plug the problem into the principle.

The great challenge of life is understanding life. When life throws us a curve ball, we often just play games and fake it. Many times, we have to guess and then wonder endlessly if our guesses will work.

What we lack is understanding. David, the great king of Israel, addressed this very issue. By divine inspiration, he spoke of the moral and social chaos in his community and described the root cause of mankind's confusion, frustration, and self-destruction: *"They know nothing, they understand nothing. They walk about in darkness; all the foundations of the earth are shaken"* (Psalm 82:5).

This text declares that the reason why the people of the earth are so confused and filled with problems is not because there are no answers but because we don't understand our Creator. We don't know His principles, His purpose, His nature, or His precepts.

Three Things That Cause Problems in Life

Psalm 82:5 identifies three progressive components that are the source of our suffering in life. First, there is a lack of knowledge—*"they know nothing."* Second, there is a misunderstanding or misconception of life—*"they understand nothing"* and cannot comprehend their environment. And third, there is a lack of spiritual sight—*"they walk about in darkness"*; they see nothing. The word *"darkness"* in the original Hebrew connotes the principle of ignorance. In most cases, its use implies the absence of knowledge. In this context, its use denotes that men are ignorant or blind to God's principles. If you attempt to live and solve the challenges of life from a position of ignorance, then you are walking in darkness and will experience exasperation, frustration, and failure.

The text concludes that the result of ignorance and a lack of understanding is that *"all the foundations of the earth are shaken."* *Foundation* implies the fundamental principles and laws that regulate function or operation. In essence, when people lack knowledge and understanding of the basic, fundamental laws of God, all life goes off track and ends in failure.

When you lack understanding, you will continually use the wrong formula. Knowledge, wisdom, and understanding, then, are vital keys to teaching the right answer.

What Is Understanding?

Here's a simple definition of understanding: "Understanding is knowledge and comprehension of the original purpose and intent of a thing and of the principles by which a thing was designed to function."

To possess understanding of something, you must know the original intent for it. First, what was in the mind of the one who made it? Second, how did the creator of a product intend it to function?

Understanding is comprehension of the truth. Why is this important? Because nothing is truly yours until you understand it. No matter how much you sit and listen, if you don't understand a thing, it's still not yours. You will never truly own or possess a thing that you do not understand. That's why information does not guarantee knowledge. Jesus Christ, the greatest Teacher of all time, said, *"He who has ears, let him hear"* (Matthew 11:15). He was separating people who simply listen to information from those who actually understand it. When you understand a thing, it becomes yours. Most of our lives are exercises in misunderstanding. We live from the blind side, and for most of us, that encompasses all sides.

Let's take this one step further: if you don't understand yourself, you don't yet possess yourself. That is why people who don't know who they are imitate other people and become someone other than who they were created to be. If you don't know what you were born to be and do, then you become the victim of other people's opinions. Understanding who made you and who you are is crucial so that others do not take possession of your life. When you have understanding, you know what to do with your life.

When I finally learned those algebraic formulas, I knew what to do with any figure given to me. This principle is so important. Again, once you understand life, it doesn't matter what life throws at you; you can work out the problem.

In this book, we are going to learn the purpose, principles, and functions of fatherhood so that it doesn't matter what the facts of your life currently are. You will know, understand, and learn how to recognize the qualities, character, and function of a true father. Facts will always submit to principles when principles show up. But if you have facts without principles, facts are going to control and frustrate your life.

Life is complicated only to a man ignorant of principles, for principles are designed to simplify life. Principles are permanent. Principles protect products. Principles preserve. Principles contain inherent judgment. Principles cannot be broken; rather, you break yourself on them. Principles do not show favoritism. Principles are independent of culture, race, or creed. Principles are the principal thing, and obedience to principles guarantees success.

Part 1

==

THE MALE'S PRIORITY AND POSITION

Chapter 1

THE PURPOSE OF
FATHERHOOD

A key theme that runs through all my books is that *purpose is inherent in everything that has been created.* I have spent thirty years studying the concepts of purpose and potential, as well as counseling and guiding thousands of individuals to live lives of personal fulfillment and social and spiritual well-being. The knowledge and experience I have gained has led me to the conclusion that the central principle of life is *purpose.* Exploring the concept of purpose leads us to an understanding of all aspects of our lives. We see an illustration of this in the way purpose guides the development of products in the business world. When a manufacturer creates a new product, the product's intended use and purpose govern the design of that product.

The priority of purpose has its origins in our Creator, and it has signifcant practical applications for us as human beings. When our Creator made humanity, He designed men and women to fulfill their specific functions and gave them qualities and characteristics to enable them to perform His intended purpose. From an analysis of Scripture, we can see that God created the male with a particular purpose in mind. He intended men to be *fathers;* therefore, He designed them to be so.

As we will see, "fatherhood" has a much broader meaning than just the biological production of children. Fatherhood is not a choice for a male but is inherent in his very nature. The essence of the male is fatherhood. *Every* adult male is meant to be a father, and his personal fulfillment is linked to living out that purpose.

Purpose is the source of all true fulfillment and defines one's existence. Without purpose, life ceases to be an existence becomes a mere experiment. If men do not know, understand, or fulfill their God-given purpose, then problems will arise both in their identity and their relationships.

Let's explore the implications of the principles of purpose and how they relate to the male's purpose of fatherhood.

The Principles of Purpose

Purpose is defined as the "original intent and reason" for the creation of a thing. Through my exploration of this most important issue, I have identified seven principles of purpose to assist you in better understanding the nature of life:

1. God is a God of purpose.
2. Everything in life has a purpose.
3. Not every purpose is known by human beings.
4. Where purpose is not known, abuse is inevitable.
5. If you want to know the purpose of a thing, never ask the thing itself.
6. Purpose is found only in the mind of the maker of the thing.
7. Purpose is the key to fulfillment.

Many of the problems males face come from a lack of understanding their own purpose in life. Principles one and two assure you that you do have a purpose on this earth. Without an understanding of God's purpose for you, however, you will abuse your life and, most likely, the lives of those around you. The solution is not to try to conjure up a purpose for yourself but to discover your Maker's original intent for you, because your purpose is found in the mind of your Maker. The great news is that discovering and living out that purpose is the key to your fulfillment as a male, a son, a brother, a husband, a father, a member of your church, a citizen in your community and nation, and a human being in the world.

The Male's Purpose

With these principles of purpose in mind, let us now turn our attention to the concept of the "Fatherhood Principle" and how it relates to the male's purpose.

We have seen that everything was created to fulfill a purpose and was designed according to the demand of that purpose. The unique difference in design that distinguishes each created thing from another is mandated and is critical to the function it is expected to perform. In essence, the difference between the physical, mental, psychological, and dispositional nature of the male and female is providential, essential, valuable, and necessary for the fulfillment of their particular purposes in life. The nature of a thing is determined by its purpose.

I want to give you the purpose of fatherhood according to the "Manufacturer's Manual" (the Bible). Understanding the purpose for the male is a critical and necessary step in understanding fatherhood, because the male was designated (*design*-ated) a father by the Creator. God was thinking "father" when He created man. As a matter of fact, buried in every boy is the potential of being a father. This means that God intends every boy to grow up into fatherhood. Again, I am not just talking about the male's biological ability to father offspring. Being a "father" is rooted in God's image because God is Father. He is not satisfied until the father comes out of the boy. Fatherhood is the design and destiny of the male.

What Is Father?

We should begin with the meaning of *father* because one of the greatest dangers to society is the misconception of what fatherhood is. Definitions determine interpretations; thus, we must start here. In the Old Testament, the Hebrew word for "father" is *ab. Abba*, meaning "Daddy," comes from this word. In the New Testament, the Greek word for father is *pater*. So, you have *ab* and *abba* in Old Testament Hebrew and *pater* in New Testament Greek.

What do *ab* and *pater* mean? These words denote very basic concepts that include the following:

- Source
- Nourisher
- Sustainer
- Supporter
- Founder
- Protector

The source of a thing is its *ab* or father. As the source, the *ab* sustains and maintains. Another aspect of the meaning of the word *father* is "upholder." Father is the source that upholds everything that comes from it.

There are some other English words related to *ab* and *pater* that describe fatherhood and are absolutely essential to the purpose of a father. Don't skim over the following words; they are loaded with meaning:

Progenitor

This term comes from the Latin meaning "to beget forth." It also denotes "precurser" or "originator." A father is the initiator or source. Generations come from the *ab* and *pater*—the father—not the mother. God created man to be father—the progenitor, source, and supporter of generations. The *ab* generates everything. That's why there is no seed in women; the male is designed as progenitor.

Ancestor. Ab also refers to ancestor.[5] The English words *ancestor* and *ancestry* ultimately come from the same Latin verb *antecedere,* meaning "to go before" or "precede." At the start of an ancestral line is the father. He begins the heritage for all his seed. This is very important. The man (father) was given the responsibility not only to start and provide the future generation, but also to give that generation an identity.

> Being a "father" is rooted in God's image because God is Father.

---

[5] See *Strong's Exhaustive Concordance,* #H1 and the New American Standard Exhaustive Concordance of the Bible (NASC), The Lockman Foundation, #H1. Used by permission.

For example, when a child is born, it normally takes its father's last name, not its mother's name. When you use both names, you are attempting to claim and produce two generations and two identities instead of one. This causes much confusion in the offspring.

In Scripture, there is no such thing as the son of two fathers. God always speaks of lineage to one man—the father. James, the son of Zebedee, was Zebedee's son, not the son of Zebedee's wife's father. Why is that important? Because the minute you start bringing in another ancestry or lineage, you split the fatherhood. There can be only one source. That is why the Bible says, *"For this reason a **man** will leave his father and mother..."* (Matthew 19:5, emphasis added). When a woman marries, her husband fulfills the roles of sustainer and supporter and so on, which her father once fulfilled.

Hard to understand? Then consider this very carefully: the wife doesn't carry her husband's father's name. She takes on whatever the husband is called. Why? All men are fathers. It's tough being a man, because whomever you marry becomes your "offspring," so to speak. That's what God intended, and that's why wives take on their husbands' names. The husband becomes responsible for his wife one hundred percent. He provides, sustains, nourishes, upholds, and supports. Jesus Himself is never referred to as the "Son of Mary" in Scripture, but rather as the "Son of God." *"The Holy Spirit will come upon you, and the power of the Most High will overshadow you. So the holy one to be born will be called the Son of God"* (Luke 1:35).

I know that Jesus was single, but He understood the principle of marriage as explained in Matthew 19. That's why, when the disciples learned this principle from Jesus, they said it was better to stay single! (See verse 10.) When you marry a woman, you are not taking on some sex object. You are not taking on someone to brag about, saying, "That's my woman." No, that's your *wife*, whom you have committed to sustain and support spiritually, emotionally, and physically. Even the bride of Christ, the church, has the name of her Bridegroom—she is called "the body of Christ." Jesus stressed, "In My name you will ask the Father everything." (See John 15:16.) We have too many husbands who are not the *ab* or *pater* that God calls men to be to their wives.

Founder

The concept of father also includes "founder" or "foundation." That's why companies, institutions, and movements use the word *father* to describe the person who established the organization, institution, or movement. The men who established the United States of America are referred to as the "Founding Fathers." Nelson Mandela is known as the "Father of the New South Africa." If someone founded something, he is called the father of it. Why? He generated it. He caused the genesis of it. God built the male to found future generations and to be the foundation on which they develop. It is essential to note that the quality of a foundation determines the value of what is built upon it.

Author

Father also implies authorship, as well as the legitimate authority of something. "Father" possesses inherent authority.

[Jesus] *is the image of the invisible God, the firstborn over all creation. For by him all things were created: things in heaven and on earth, visible and invisible, whether thrones or powers or rulers or authorities; all things were created by him and for him.* (Colossians 1:15–16)

The triune God in Christ Jesus is the *"author of eternal salvation"* (Hebrews 5:9 KJV) and the *"author and finisher of our faith"* (Hebrews 12:2 KJV). What does it mean to be the *"author of eternal salvation"*? Jesus initiated, generated, produced, upholds, and sustains the salvation of all mankind. He is the sole Source of our redemption.

If you want to come to God, therefore, Jesus is the ultimate Source. That's why, despite the works of Mohammed, Buddha, and Confucius, you can't go to any of those men for salvation; according to Scripture, they didn't generate, create, or author mankind's redemption. Jesus is the Generator of salvation; it germinated with Him and it is completed in Him. He is both the Author and Finisher of our faith.

> **God is our Father in two main ways: through creation and through redemption.**

I'm so glad He's not just the Author, but also the Finisher. Many men are merely authors of babies; they don't finish as fathers. Jesus is a good Daddy. He's the Finisher of your faith. He didn't just start your faith; He'll see it to the end until it is complete. He will cause you to grow up to the full measure of His purpose for you so that you look just like Him. (See 2 Corinthians 3:18; Ephesians 4:13.)

Jesus provides the "gene" for the new generation of man. He is the Source of seed for salvation. All fathers provide the genes or "seed" that determine the attributes of the generations they produce. In Isaiah's description of the Messiah, he concluded with the titles Wonderful Counselor, Mighty God, *Everlasting Father,* and Prince of Peace. (See Isaiah 9:6.) How did the Son become Father? He produced a new generation of human beings. He became the *"last Adam"* (1 Corinthians 15:45) or the *"second man"* (v. 47) who produced the *"new man"* (Ephesians 2:15).

Teacher

Father is also the one who teaches and nourishes. This means he provides nutrients and resources that develop, enrich, expand, grow, and deploy that which comes from him. One of man's major responsibilities is to teach his "offspring." Many men are found lacking in this area of teaching and are intimidated by the women they marry. Let me tell you something: the male is wired to teach, so you don't need to know much about teaching techniques. Males, by nature, love to give instruction. The father-instinct of teaching is inherent within them. Incidentally, this is why men often resist the attempts women make to instruct them. If you're a man, you're a teacher. Get knowledge and understanding from God's Word so that you can effectively fulfill this role:

> *For the* LORD *gives wisdom, and from his mouth come knowledge and understanding.* (Proverbs 2:6)

> *Blessed is the man who finds wisdom, the man who gains understanding.* (Proverbs 3:13)

> *Get wisdom, get understanding; do not forget my words or swerve from them.* (Proverbs 4:5)

Some men are so ignorant that when they come into the presence of a well-educated woman, they feel threatened. You must get knowledge and understanding from the Word of God so you can lead your family with wisdom, knowledge, integrity, and confidence.

Creator. Father also denotes "creator." We saw earlier with the word *founder* that father is one who founds something. The same concept applies to the creation and invention of things; we refer to people who create things as the father of them. For example, Thomas Edison, the inventor of the lightbulb, is known as the "father of the lightbulb."

Father Is a Title Relating to Function

Jesus taught us to pray, *"Our Father which art in heaven, hallowed be thy name"* (Matthew 6:9 KJV). Isaiah 63:16 declares, *"But you are our Father, though Abraham does not know us or Israel acknowledge us; you, O LORD, are our Father, our Redeemer from of old is your name."* When we use the term *Our Father* in relation to God, we must remember that this is not so much a name as a title resulting from a function. We can say that God is our Father in two main ways: through creation and through redemption.

Father as the Source of Creation

First, God is the Source and Sustainer of everything He created, which makes Him the Father of all things; He is the Father of creation. Malachi 2:10 says, *"Have we not all one Father? Did not one God create us? Why do we profane the covenant of our fathers by breaking faith with one another?"* God is called Father rather than Mother. Why? It has to do with function. He is the Source and Sustainer. Everything came from Him, but He Himself did not come from any other source. The word

God means self-sustaining, self-sufficient One. God is life and gives everything life.

Hebrews 12:9 reveals that God is *"the Father of spirits"* (KJV). Why? *"God is a Spirit"* (John 4:24 KJV). He is the Source of all spirits because He created them all. Whatever God creates comes out of Him. Whether it is material or spirit, God is still the Father of it. He is Father by virtue of His creative will. James 1:17 reveals that God is *"the Father of the heavenly lights."* That means stars, suns, moons, and everything that exists in the universe came out of God. He is the Father of all that is.

The feminist movement says, "We've got to change the Bible. The Bible is male chauvinistic because it refers to God only as 'Him' and 'He' and 'Father.'" To address this issue, some Bibles have been published that adjust the Scriptures to have more inclusive language. Instead of *Father*, God is called *Our Divine One*. Instead of *him* or *her, one* is used. For example, Jude 24 might read, "Now unto the one who is able to keep us from falling." Or they might even say, "The Lord is my Shepherdess."

What they and many others don't understand is God's nature. His very essence is "Father." Why? He's the Source of creation. He's the Creator of all things; therefore, He's Father. It comes with having the seed. If you produce the seed, you are the father. So the term *Father* is not just something bestowed upon God; it's the natural result of His creating everything. All of us came out of God, the Father.

Father as the Source of Redemption

God is also our Father through our redemption in Jesus Christ. In chapter four, we will explore the relationship of Jesus to the Father in more detail. But let us note here that as the Son of God, Jesus continually referred to God as His Father. Through His sinless life and sacrifice on the cross, He restored fallen mankind—who had rebelled against their Creator and been cut off from fellowship with Him—to their heavenly Father. After Jesus' resurrection, He said to His disciples, *"I ascend unto **my** Father, and **your** Father; and to my God, and your God"* (John 20:17, emphasis added). We can call the Creator our Father again because of the redemption provided through Christ.

As we saw earlier, Jesus Himself is called "Father." Look again at the powerful revelation given about Jesus:

> *For to us a **child** is born, to us a son is given, and the government will be on his shoulders. And he will be called Wonderful Counselor, Mighty God, **Everlasting Father**, Prince of Peace.* (Isaiah 9:6, emphasis added)

How is it that the child went from being the Son to being the Father? It is because Jesus and the Father are one. (See John 10:30.) Ephesians 1:3 declares that God is *"the God and Father of our Lord Jesus Christ."* When the Son showed up on Earth, He came from the Father, but they are one. The Father and the Son are one! In John 1:1, we read concerning Jesus, *"In the beginning was the Word, and the Word was with God, and the Word was God."* For His atonement purposes, Jesus is the Son, but when it comes to His function and responsibility, He's *"Everlasting Father."*

For example, when the religious leaders started to talk to Jesus about their forefather Abraham, they said, in essence, "We know who our father is." They tried to put Jesus down by saying He didn't know who His Father was. They were implying, "You're illegitimate. You were conceived out of wedlock. You don't know who Your father is. We know who our father is; our father is Abraham." Jesus answered, "Don't you know that before Abraham was, I am?" In other words, "Abraham came out of Me; I am Abraham's Father." (See John 8.) It's tough to tell God anything about being a father; after all, He is *Abba*—the Source of all created things.

The Son is the essence, the very being, of the Father. The early Christians understood this. At the Council of Nicea (325 A.D.), they affirmed,

> We believe in one God, the Father almighty, maker of all things, visible and invisible;
>
> And in one Lord Jesus Christ, the Son of God, *begotten from the Father,* only-begotten, *that is, from the substance of the Father,* God from God, light from light, *true God from true God, begotten not made, of one substance with the Father,* through Whom all things came into being, things in heaven and things on earth.[6]

You cannot be a true father unless you are willing to uphold that which comes out of you. God sustains everything that has come out of Him. Through the Son, God the Father made all the worlds and upholds all things by the power of His Word.

> *In these last days he has spoken to us by his Son, whom he appointed heir of all things, and through whom he made the universe. The Son is the radiance of God's glory and the exact representation of his being, **sustaining all things by his powerful word.** After he had provided purification for sins, he sat down at the right hand of the Majesty in heaven.* (Hebrews 1:2–3, emphasis added)

---

[6] Linwood Urban, *A Short History of Christian Thought* (New York: Oxford University Press, 1995), 64 (italicized words are author's emphasis).

In the Image of the Father

With this understanding of father as source and sustainer, let us begin to see how God created the male to be father on earth. Acts 17:26 reads, *"From one man he made every nation of men, that they should inhabit the whole earth."* Adam was created first (see Genesis 2:7–8, 18–23), and it was from him that all humanity, including Eve, came. That is why, in the genealogy of Jesus recorded in Luke 3, the lineage concludes with, *"...the son of Seth, the son of Adam, the son of God"* (v. 38). Adam came from God. In essence, the source is also the *abba*, the father.

Note that in the creation record in Genesis, God created only one human being from the soil. He never went back to the soil to create Eve or any other human being. He placed all of mankind in that first man, Adam. This is a mystery. Everything God wanted for the human race was in that one man. God went to the soil, carved out one male, breathed life into him, created out of that male a female, and then said, "Now be fruitful." (See Genesis 1:28.)

> Every man, whether married or not, has the inherent identity and purpose of fatherhood.

In that one man, Adam, was the potential for every other male and female in history. Why? Because God wanted Adam to be the source of all people, and He designed the male to be the father. The male is father, not by vote or cultural positioning, but by virtue of his disposition in the process of creation. This is because he—the human *ab* and *pater*—was to represent God. God the Father is the perfect Model, Example, and Mentor for all men who desire to be true fathers.

Just as God is the Father of all living things, He made man to be the father of the human family. Every man is created with the responsibility of fatherhood. Every male carries with him millions of sperm because he is the "source." Men have been prepared by God to be fathers.

This is why every man, whether married or not, has the inherent identity and purpose of fatherhood. Fatherhood is not necessarily related to having a baby. You're destined to be a father by the simple fact that you're a male. If you are a male, then you are responsible for anything that comes out of you. Because Eve was created from Adam, you are responsible for the female and any offspring that comes out of the female. Paul referred to this principle and responsibility of the male as the primary source of the human family:

> *Now I want you to realize that the head of every man is Christ, and the head of the woman is man, and the head of Christ is God....For man did not come from woman, but woman from man. In the Lord, however, woman is not independent of man, nor is man independent of woman.*
>
> (1 Corinthians 11:3, 8, 11)

God created the man to be the father of the family. That's why He made the male first.

The Principles of Fatherhood

A principle is a fundamental law that governs function and behavior. We must understand the basic laws of fatherhood in order to be effective fathers. The father is the source that sustains, protects, nourishes, and provides identity for that which he produces. Men are therefore distinguished in their role of father by the following principles:

The male is the source of seed. The male is the host of the sperm. He is the source of human life, whereas the woman is the incubator of life. It is the woman who gives life to the man's seed.

The male is the nourisher of fruit. The seed of a tree gets planted, and then it becomes another tree that bears fruit.

> **The father is the source that sustains, protects, nourishes, and provides identity for that which he produces.**

Whatever comes out of the seed is fruit; therefore you, as a father, are responsible for nourishing the fruit. The seed supplies the tree that sustains the fruit that, in turn, produces more seed. Father means nourisher.

The male is the source of the female. First Corinthians 11:8 says, *"For man did not come from woman, but woman from man."* Therefore, the glory of the man is the woman. (See verse 7.) In other words, the man is responsible for what came out of him. Since woman came from man, men are responsible for women and how they treat them. If you are a young man who is dating a young woman, you are to treat her with respect, as you would want someone to treat your own daughter. You are not to pressure her into sexual intercourse before marriage. When a woman goes out with a man, she's supposed to feel protected physically, emotionally, and spiritually.

The male is designed to protect his fruit. That's the reason for your strength, men. God gave men physical strength and physique. Their bone structure is heavier and bigger than the woman's—not to beat her but to protect her. Many men kick, slap, and curse their wives, and they think they're real men. They are not real men; they are imposters and fools ignorant of their God-given purpose. Such ignorant men are dangerous because where purpose is not known, abuse is inevitable. The safest place for a woman should be in the arms of her husband. If she can't be safe there, she's in trouble.

Remember, whatever comes out of you is a part of you. If a man hates his wife, then he also hates himself. *"'A man will leave his father and mother and be united to his wife, and the two will become one flesh.' So they are no longer two, but one"* (Mark 10:7–8). God's Word says to love your wife as yourself. (See Ephesians 5:25–33.) If a man loves his wife, he loves his own flesh. A man who walks around slapping, kicking, and cursing himself is considered crazy. Fatherhood is an awesome responsibility because you are the progenitor of all that comes out of you and must protect all that comes out of you. Father means protector.

The male determines the type of the offspring and influences its quality. Because you carry the seed within you, you carry the type of "tree" your offspring will become. You also have the power to influence the eventual quality of that tree by your character. So I say this to all women: Be careful about the type of seed you receive in your soil. There are some bad seeds. Some men walking around look like good fruit, but they're really just gooseberries. When a woman thinks about marriage, she should make sure she understands the nature and quality of her prospective mate. Whatever you receive, you will produce. Whatever you sow, you will reap. (See Galatians 6:7.)

Men, you also must be careful about what kind of soil you use to plant your seed. The seed may be good, but if the soil has poor nutrients in it, then you will have a sick tree. Good seed should never be strewn about just anywhere. You want quality soil for your seed in order to guarantee good trees. The quality of the woman affects the quality of the fruit. Fatherhood means quality management.

The male maintains his offspring. The fatherhood principle is to maintain. The male is responsible for the security, sustenance, and development of his seed. Fatherhood means maintenance.

The male teaches his seed. A male is a godly father when he takes responsibility for his seed and gives his seed knowledge. The source must train and instruct the resource. That is fatherhood. Most women are doing the teaching and the training, but God says that fathers are to do the primary spiritual teaching and training in the home. That means you, as the male, are responsible not only for having babies, but also for training those babies and teaching them to walk in the ways of the Lord.

It's difficult to lead children to the Lord if you are an absentee father. It's hard to take people to where God is if you are not heading that way yourself. You cannot lead your family to a place where you are not going.

These, then, are the primary principles of fatherhood. Are you ready to become the father God created you to be? Do you know what a father is to do? Do you know how a father should talk and act? In the next two chapters, we will look at some pictures of what it means to be a father to those for whom you are responsible in life. Then we will take a look at ten specific functions of fatherhood.

CHAPTER PRINCIPLES

1. Purpose is inherent in everything that has been created.

2. The difference between the physical, mental, psychological, and dispositional nature of the male and female is providential, essential, valuable, and necessary for the fulfillment of their particular purposes in life.

3. God intended men to be fathers; therefore, He designed them to be so.

4. Father denotes Source, Nourisher, Sustainer, Supporter, Founder, and Protector. It also means Progenitor, Ancestor, Founder, Author, Teacher, and Creator.

5. *Father* is not so much a name but a title resulting from a function. God is our Father through our creation and our redemption in Jesus Christ. God is the Source of all creation, and we are restored to Him as Father through the sacrifice of His Son Jesus, the "Everlasting Father" who produced a new generation of human beings.

6. Jesus, God the Son, is the essence, the very being, of the Father.

7. Just as God is the Father of all living things, He made Adam to be the father of the human family.

8. Men are distinguished in their role of father in the following ways: the male is the source of seed; the male is the nourisher of fruit; the male is the source of the female; the male is designed to protect his fruit; the male determines the type of the offspring and influences its quality; the male maintains his offspring; the male teaches his seed.

Chapter 2

THE MALE AS FOUNDATION AND ANCHOR

M en were created to be source and sustainer. They are the underpining not only for their homes, but also for their churches, communities, and nations. Being source and sustainer doesn't mean that you lord it over others, or that you necessarily run things. It means you are *responsible* for everything.

The Male as Foundation

The kingdom of God teaches that the male is the foundation of the house—he carries everything. As a husband, you are the foundation of your marriage. As a father, you are the foundation of your home. As a pastor, you are the foundation of your ministry.

Fatherhood is God's way of building and sustaining the human family. His plan is to fulfill His vision of the earth as an extension of His heavenly kingdom. This happens as the male functions as the foundation of the home, allowing all those he is responsible for the protection and freedom to grow and prosper as God intended, for His glory and the expansion of His ways on the earth.

In the Introduction, I discussed the result of our ignorance and lack of understanding about the nature of fatherhood, based on the words of Psalm 82:5: *"They know nothing, they understand nothing. They walk about in darkness; all the foundations of the earth are shaken."* Darkness implies ignorance. A lack of knowledge and understanding promotes ignorance, which jeopardizes the very foundations of society. *"Foundation"* in the above verse implies the fundamental principles and laws that regulate function or operation. When people lack knowledge and understanding of the basic, fundamental laws of God, all life goes off track and ends in failure. True fatherhood is the way to re-secure the foundations of our societies.

> **Men, you're the foundation of your family, and a building is only as secure as its foundation.**

Let us look at the human family—and society, by extension—as a building. The key to constructing any building is the structure's foundation, because the foundation carries the weight of the building. Remember that the quality of a foundation determines the stability and value of what is built upon it. God built the male to found future generations and to be the foundation on which they develop. Having the qualities of a strong foundation is therefore essential for every man.

There are 6.7 billion people on earth today, and, as I wrote earlier, God created only one from the soil; all the rest came from that one man. God built a human family structure, and at the bottom, he laid only one foundation—the male. The human race did not begin with a couple. We frequently hear people say that God built the human race on the family. That's not exactly accurate. He started with a male on the bottom as the foundation.

We have seen that all of humanity came from Adam. Yet the male is the foundation in another way, as well. Note that it was to Adam alone that God gave instructions for work on earth and for what could and could not be done. It was only after this that Eve was created.

The Lord God took the man and put him in the Garden of Eden to work it and take care of it. And the Lord God commanded the man, "You are free to eat from any tree in the garden; but you must not eat from the tree of the knowledge of good and evil, for when you eat of it you will surely die." The Lord God said, "It is not good for the man to be alone. I will make a helper suitable for him."...So the Lord God caused the man to fall into a deep sleep; and while he was sleeping, he took one of the man's ribs and closed up the place with flesh. Then the Lord God made a woman from the rib he had taken out of the man, and he brought her to the man. The man said, "This is now bone of my bones and flesh of my flesh; she shall be called 'woman,' for she was taken out of man." (Genesis 2:15–18, 21–23)

God did not give any instructions to the female, but only to the male. All the information was given to the man to teach to those who came after him. Please keep in mind that I am referring to function according to creation. The male's function as foundation is not an excuse to exert control over others:

In the Lord, however, woman is not independent of man, nor is man independent of woman. For as woman came from man, so also man is born of woman. But everything comes from God. (1 Corinthians 11:11–12)

Cracks in the Foundation Lead to Disaster

Whether you like it or not, men, you're the foundation of your family, and a building is only as secure as its foundation. A building can have a number of problems and not be condemned according to the code of a city. But if a crack is discovered in the foundation of a building, it doesn't matter how nice the interior is, the building will need serious repair and may well be condemned, and then no one can use it.

God laid men as the foundation of the family, and we need to be careful not to allow any cracks in our character. If you see a crack developing, fix it immediately! Do not let it get any bigger, or the whole structure may collapse. You may think that character lapses affect only you, but they also affect those entrusted to your protection, teaching, and care. Evaluate the current state of your character and take steps to correct what you see. In doing so, you will strengthen your entire family.

A Foundation Functions without Being Seen

Where is the foundation of a building located? At the bottom. You can see the walls, the doors, the lighting, and the furnishings of a building, but you can't see the foundation once it is laid and the building is built upon it. Likewise, as the foundation, men are to do what they have to do for those around them without drawing attention to themselves.

You don't see the foundation. Why? It's too busy carrying everything. Real men do not advertise their responsibility.

Real men do not go around telling everyone including their wives what they're doing for them. Real men do not pronounce to the community what they're doing for their families. You just see the family functioning well and working together. The English word *husband* is derived from an Old Norse word meaning *householder.* We can say that the husband is meant to "hold the house" intact. He's the glue that keeps his family together. Likewise, a good pastor doesn't tell the church members everything he's doing for them; the community just sees or experiences the results of his work.

> Men are supposed to "fasten" the society—to secure it with beliefs and principles that don't change.

Don't ever tell your children what you're doing for them. Don't throw in your wife's face what you're doing for her. After all, she was probably doing fine in her parents' house. Real men are quiet about it. They just carry the responsibility.

The most important part of a building is the part you can't see. Become a man that your family, community, and nation can stand secure on, knowing that you won't collapse beneath them, regardless of what forces come against you.

The Male as Anchor

Men are not only the foundation, but also the anchor of the human family. An *anchor* is defined as "a reliable or principal support: mainstay" and "something that serves to hold an object firmly." Another definition is "anything that gives stability and security." You need stability and security in an environment that is unstable and insecure. That is a description of the world we live in.

An Anchor Secures and Brings Rest

As a verb, *to anchor* means "to fasten, to stop, or to rest." Those three words are a great description of fatherhood. Men are supposed to "fasten" the society—to secure it with beliefs and principles that don't change. The male is also supposed to stop things from happening that are harmful to others. I sometimes think it is amazing what we allow to happen. As anchors, we can stop our families from being swept away by the currents of immorality, stabilize uncertain youth, and bring safety and order back to communities. The anchor also brings rest—when people have a true anchor present in their lives, they experience an inner peace.

You should think of your family as a ship, and you as the anchor of that ship. A ship has no foundation of its own. The hull, the masts, the sails, the rigging, and even the helm can't fulfill that function. Your boat may look beautiful on the outside; yet, by itself, it contains no foundation. The only thing that secures a boat is an anchor. When the anchor is in place, the entire hull comes to rest. Even if the ship is beaten, twisted, and torn by waves, a strong anchor keeps it from breaking apart and allows it to weather the storms.

An Anchor Is Tested during Storms

It doesn't matter how much you brag about the strength of an anchor; the only way it will be truly tested is during intense pressure. When I was growing up in the Bahamas, where I still live, my friends and I had a little boat called a

Boston Whaler. We worked during the summers and bought our own boat with our earnings. We would go out and water ski every day after school. I loved waterskiing and the feeling of flying over the ocean.

One day, we went to the back of Rose Island and were skiing when we decided we wanted to do a little diving off a reef. We found a rock, and we put the anchor on it, but the current was so strong that it pulled the anchor and actually broke it. Now we were in danger; we had a boat without an anchor in a current. Fortunately, the current carried the boat to where we were able to get home safely. But the experience emphasized for me that having an anchor is not enough. Your anchor must be able to handle the rough currents and storms of life.

There are hazardous social and cultural forces and unexpected setbacks that will control the course of your life if you have not discovered how to be a strong anchor. You must realize that if you break under pressure, your "ship" will become a victim of these currents and storms. Just as it is not enough merely to say your boat has a strong anchor, it is not good enough just to say, "I am a man." You have to ask, "What kind of man am I? What currents and storms am I really able to handle?"

You can be sure that the first decision my friends and I made when we returned home was to buy a new, strong anchor because we knew we couldn't go out in our boat again without one. Don't go out into the world without having your anchor already in place. Having a strong anchor takes away the fear of the current.

Here is some reassurance from our great Creator through the apostle Paul:

No temptation has seized you except what is common to man. And God is faithful; he will not let you be tempted beyond what you can bear. But when you are tempted, he will also provide a way out so that you can stand up under it. (1 Corinthians 10:13)

It doesn't matter what comes against you or what unexpected problems arise. Maybe your plans for your life or your family fell apart. Perhaps things have happened to you that you didn't foresee. Keep in mind God's promise. He would not have allowed them if you were not able to overcome them through His strength. God will verify your quality as an anchor by how you respond to the tests He allows to come to you.

Some of you may be saying, "But this is the worst situation I've ever experienced!" God is telling you, "No, this is the best revelation of how tough you are in Me." God would not allow you to go through it if you weren't built for it. If your test is greater than your neighbor's or your coworker's, it is because, at the moment, your anchor capacity is stronger. Otherwise, God would not allow that test.

I am personally responsible for securing a million dollars a month for operating expenses in my company. I'm not just the president; I'm the key man, to use an insurance term. I generate what happens in the company. I am able to handle this responsibility because the Creator has given me this test every month, and I have learned how to live with that kind of pressure by relying on His grace and provision. Therefore, I don't go around complaining when the money isn't there yet and asking, "Why is the devil doing this?" or "Why do I have these tough times?" I don't have any tough times; I am a tough anchor! I have been tested by the storms.

God reveals the quality of your anchorage by the level of testing He allows you to go through. So if you aren't going through much, either the quality of your mettle is still weak or you just need to wait a while; it will come. You can pray and fast all you want or donate millions to the church, but you are still going to be tested *"because you know that the testing of your faith develops perseverance. Perseverance must finish its work so that you may be mature and complete, not lacking anything"* (James 1:3–4). Let no one tell you that following Christ is a test-free ride.

Weakness Is Tested to Insure Strength

We must become men of tests. No vision is validated until it is tested. A key principle of testing is that your tests are designed by your declarations. This means that if you don't want any tests, don't declare that you're going to do anything in life. The moment you make a declaration that you're going to do something, life will test your resolve.

For example, if a man says, "I am not going to have sex before marriage," every old girlfriend of his will appear in his life within the next week. And he will wonder what happened. He just invited the test by his declaration. Or perhaps you say, "I'm going to start a business!" That declaration will be tested by obstacles and setbacks to see if you really mean it. Remember what Peter once told Jesus? *"Lord, I am ready to go with you to prison and to death"* (Luke 22:33). In other words, "Lord, I don't know about the other disciples, but as for me, I will never leave You or forsake You." Oh, no, Peter! You should have just thought that rather than declared it. Now you're in trouble. Jesus replied, in effect, "Peter, Satan has just demanded that you appear for trial on what you said. I have prayed that your faith won't fail in the midst of it, that you will still believe what I told you." (See verses 31–32.)

An anchor is tested by storms; it is only as good as what it survives. Some of you are reading this because God is going to bring you through something big, and He wants you to remember these instructions. He wants to make you aware that you are about to take on a great project He has planned for you. It may frighten you at first, but He wants you to learn to survive the little storms so you can weather the larger ones in fulfillment of the vision. God will test before He entrusts. If God is going to trust you with something and use you to accomplish it, He has to test you first.

> **God allows you to go through trials and tests in order to expose your "spots" and let Him remove them.**

While Satan may tempt us to give up when we make a declaration, the Bible says that God doesn't tempt us. He tests and refines us. What's the difference between a test and a temptation? A test is more like the act of tempering metal. The Greeks and Romans used tempering in the process of making swords for use in battle. They would take a piece of steel and put it in fire until it became so hot you could see into it and determine if there were any black spots in it. The black spots that the heat revealed were areas in which the molecules were not close enough together; they were weak areas. When spots were discovered, they would put the hot sword on a steel anvil and hit it with a steel mallet. They would strike the spots and, as they hit them, the molecules would come together. They would keep hitting the steel until they couldn't see any more spots. Then they would put the sword in cold water and the steel would harden. After that, they would put the sword back in the fire until it became hot and malleable again, and they would look for additional spots. If they found any, they would go through the process again. They would keep doing this—fire, beating, cold water—until they couldn't see any more spots.

After a sword had gone through this process, they could be sure it would not break in the middle of a battle where a soldier's life depended on it. You never trust a sword that has not been tempered. This process is similar to how God tests us. *Tempering means testing for weakness to insure strength.* God doesn't need the tempering process in order to see your true character. He can already see into you, and He knows your secret "spots." He knows your habits, your weaknesses, your unhealthy relationships, the garbage you have hidden away. He knows everything about you. The tempering is for your sake. He allows you to go through trials and tests so you can recognize what is hindering your life.

Going through a temptation can have the same result if we hold on to our faith. Again, God doesn't tempt anyone, but He will allow Satan to do so. When Jesus was taken before Caiaphas, the high priest, God allowed Satan to put pressure on Peter; as a result, when Peter was asked if he was with Jesus, he lied, "I don't know Him!" Yet recall that Jesus had told Peter beforehand, in effect, "I'm going to pray that your faith doesn't fail in the midst of that pressure, so that when you come back to Me, you can strengthen your brothers." (See Luke 22:32.) Although Peter denied Jesus, He did not lose His faith in Him; he repented, and Jesus restored him. (See John 21:15–19.)

God permits storms in order to expose your "spots." You must learn what they are and allow Him to remove them because you are only as strong as the storms you survive. Every time you survive a storm, a few more spots are beaten out of your life. The more storms you go through, the more spots that are removed. When the spots are purged, then God can call you His sword. He will hold you out as an example, saying, "This man will defend my cause. I'm not afraid that he's going to break in the middle of the fight."

Have you ever wondered why so many "Christian celebrities" crack in the middle of trials? They haven't been in the fire long enough. They wouldn't stay under the hammer! They haven't been strengthened in the water. We're meant to dream big, but we must remember that along the way, we will be put in the fire, beaten, and then put in cold water. Sometimes, as soon as we make it out of the water and think the test is over, He will put us back in the fire because we need to be refined further.

Think about the life of Abraham. The Lord told him, in essence, "Abraham, I want to trust you with a brand new nation I want to build. So I have to test you. Kill your only son, the son of promise, as a sacrifice to Me." Abraham had to have great faith in the midst of the test to believe that if he killed Isaac, God could raise him up again. He exercised this faith and passed the test. God did not want him to kill Isaac; He needed to know that Abraham would put Him before all else and trust Him to fulfill the promise in His own way and time. Likewise, God may say to you, "I want you to give Me your business this year. I want you to 'kill' it." You answer, "Oh, but God, I've worked so hard to build it!" "Give Me the business. I want to see if you love it more than you love Me. Lately, you've been spending more time in business than in church and prayer, so give Me the business this year." If you start complaining to God, He may say, "See, if I can't trust you with this, I can't trust you with bigger things."

Anchors are designed to secure a ship; that's why they must be tested. It's too late to test them in an emergency. When a ship is heading toward a rocky shore, its anchor must hold. Similarly, when your family runs into problems, *you* must hold. You have to hold that family together. If you are the oldest male living at home with your mother and sisters, and your father is absent, you are the "father" of that house. Your mother wasn't designed to fill that purpose. Jesus took over His family's leadership after Joseph died. And He made sure with His last breaths that His mother would be secured in John's household after He was gone. He was being the sustainer of His mother.

> **Anchors must be tested beforehand. It's too late to test them in an emergency.**

When the anchor of a family fails, disaster is inevitable. If you walk out on your marriage, you will not only destroy a family, but you will also damage the community. If you're a pastor, and things aren't going right, and you abandon the pulpit before God calls you to leave, you will cause problems in the body of Christ. That's not a decision affecting you only because you're called to be the anchor.

Remember that storms are only for a season. You are being tested to insure your strength as a father. You will come back from the storms better than ever, in a way others have never seen you before. Your best years are still ahead of you. It may be a seedtime right now. You've been planting, but the harvest will come. Let God refine you, and a new man will emerge.

You're an anchor. Protect your ship throughout the journey so that it can arrive at its destination safely.

CHAPTER PRINCIPLES

1. The kingdom of God teaches that the male is the foundation of the house—he carries everything.

2. God gave all the information to the man to teach to those who came after him.

3. God laid men as the foundation of the family, and they need to be careful not to allow any cracks in their character, which could lead to disaster for their families.

4. A foundation functions without being seen. As the foundation, men are to do what they have to do for those around them without drawing attention to themselves.

5. Men are not only the foundation, but also the anchor of the human family. An anchor is "a reliable or principal support: mainstay," "something that serves to hold an object firmly," and "anything that gives stability and security."

6. To anchor means "to fasten, to stop, or to rest." Anchors secure and bring rest.

7. The strength of an anchor can only be tested during intense pressure.

8. Our weaknesses are exposed through tests. In this way, we can learn what they are and allow God to remove them so we can become strong anchors.

Chapter 3

THE CORNERSTONE OF FATHERHOOD

I f you are thinking that being a foundation or an anchor is too much weight and responsibility for you, you are right. Both a foundation and an anchor need to rest on solid rock if they are going to be able to hold things up and hold things together. In the same way, it is not enough to know your function as a father; you have to know who to lean on in order to weather the storms we talked about in the previous chapter.

Build Down in order to Build Up

When I was in London for a speaking engagement a few years ago, I noticed a foundation being dug for a new hotel not far from the Millennium Dome. From my own hotel room, I could look down at the construction site. I took a photo of it for my seminars because I thought it was such a striking reminder of what it takes to build a tall building.

When you construct a building, what do you do first? You build *down*.

That's remarkable, isn't it? As I watched the men at that construction site, they kept digging and digging, and I thought, *My goodness, that hole is equivalent to about five floors below ground level.* They had to go that deep. What were they looking for?

Solid rock. In a similar way, although you are to be a stable foundation for your family, who is actually carrying the whole structure? A physical building rests on its foundation, but the foundation is resting on rock. Therefore, if you're going to be a real man, a true father, you have to be resting on the solid Rock.

The Chief Cornerstone

Now, the male is the foundation, but he is not the Rock. Who is that Rock? It is Jesus Christ. We read in Ephesians,

> *Consequently, you are no longer foreigners and aliens, but fellow citizens with God's people and members of God's household built on the foundation of the prophets and apostles, **with Christ Himself as the chief cornerstone.***"
> (Ephesians 2:19, emphasis added)

Many of us aren't familiar with how essential a cornerstone can be to a building; the way we build many of our structures today, what we call the cornerstone is usually just a facade. On one of my trips to Israel, however, I saw a clear example of what it means for Christ to be the Chief Cornerstone of our lives.

The group I was traveling with was in Caesarea and the area of Capernaum, and we went to visit an ancient synagogue, one that Jesus was said to have taught in. Being the inquisitive person I am, I wanted to learn what was underneath. I always go beyond what people tell me because I'm after education and not just information. I walked around the little synagogue, and in back there was a rock at the bottom of the foundation, so I asked our guide, who was also a Jewish rabbi, "What is that rock?" He said, "Oh, that is the chief cornerstone."

His answer made me jump, because I immediately thought of the verse from Ephesians, and I said, "Explain that to me." The rabbi said, "They lay foundations by interlocking stones." In other words, they laid the stones where they locked into each other. They didn't pour concrete in those days; they used interlocking systems. Every rock was carved in such a way that it fit into the rock next to it and they locked in place. When the foundation was nearly completed, and they were at the end of the interlocking stones, one stone had to lock into the last two stones in one corner in order to seal the whole thing together. That was the cornerstone. Without a cornerstone, the foundation would fall apart. If you want to destroy a building constructed in this way, all you have to do is move the cornerstone.

> You can't build your life on shifting sand. You need to dig down deep and find the solid Rock.

As a male, you are God's foundation for your family, but it's an interlocking foundation that needs something to hold it secure. Jesus Christ Himself is the only hope for your survival as a father because He's the Chief Cornerstone.

Men all over the world are creating businesses and industries, amassing wealth, contructing houses, making ships and aircraft, and so on. They are building, building, building, but their lives are falling apart—their wives are leaving them, their kids are on drugs, they themselves are drug addicts or alcoholics, and they don't have any sense of what is really important in life. They have much wealth, but everything is coming apart because they lack a vital relationship with God and they're missing the Chief Cornerstone. If you were to be completely honest, some of you reading this book would have to admit that you haven't wanted Jesus Christ in your life. Yet you need Him! He is essential to your life. Stop treating Him as if He is optional.

When we dedicate a school, a church, or another building, we often put a little plaque on the bottom corner of the building. That's the ceremonial cornerstone. It's not a real cornerstone such as the one I just described, but the practice comes from placing an actual cornerstone. Whose name goes on a cornerstone? Many times, it is the builder's name. If you go to Greece and Rome today, you can still see who built many of the ancient buildings because the name of the contractor is carved in the cornerstone.

It doesn't matter how important, talented, or rich you think you are. Who's holding you together? Whose name is on your cornerstone? If it's Buddha, Muhammad, Confucius, Scientology, secularism, humanism, atheism, materialism—whatever it is—rather than Jesus Christ, I can tell the future of your building. It will ultimately fall. But the Scripture assures us, *"See, I lay a stone in Zion, a chosen and precious cornerstone, and the one who trusts in him will never be put to shame"* (1 Peter 2:6).

Like the construction workers building the hotel, you can't build your life on ground that shifts when it encounters too much pressure. You need to dig down deep and find the solid Rock. As Jesus said,

> *I will show you what he is like who comes to me and hears my words and puts them into practice. He is like a man*

building a house, who dug down deep and laid the founda-
tion on rock. When a flood came, the torrent struck that
house but could not shake it, because it was well built. But
the one who hears my words and does not put them into
practice is like a man who built a house on the ground with-
out a foundation. The moment the torrent struck that house,
it collapsed and its destruction was complete.

(Luke 6:47–49)

Anchored on the Rock

There is a concept equivalent to the cornerstone in the analogy of the anchor. For about twelve years in a row, every Saturday at 5:00 a.m., my associates and I would head out to sea in our boat and go spear fishing. We caught our own fish every weekend, and our wives loved it because we never had to go out and buy seafood. We became very close because we'd have to watch each other's backs for sharks and other dangers when we were out in the water. We knew we might run into a strong current or storm, but because we had an anchor on board, we didn't feel anxious about it.

The word *Bahamas* means "shallow waters," but there's a place where the sea drops off about six thousand feet, which is called the tongue of the ocean. One time four of us, as well as the wife of one of the men, went out fishing. We were diving at a reef right next to the tongue. As long as we stayed in the shallow area, the boat's anchor held because it could reach rock at the bottom. But then we inadvertently put the anchor down in some sand, and the current from the tongue of the ocean started dragging the boat. We didn't realize it, however, and the captain of the boat was also unaware of the problem.

When the boat drifted over the tongue, the anchor really had nothing to hold on to; it was thousands of feet above the bottom of the ocean. When we noticed what was happening, we told the captain, and he tried to start the engine, but the engine wouldn't start! The boat was drifting over the depths of the ocean.

That was a moment I'll never forget. Here we were, being pulled by a strong current, our only refuge was that boat, and the boat wouldn't start. We prayed, "Oh, God, please let the engine start!" At that point, the boat's anchor was useless as our security because it had nothing to hold on to, and it was a victim of the current.

Night fell, and it was pitch black over the ocean; we couldn't see anything around us, we had no idea where we were, and we were still drifting. Let me tell you, among the four of us there were a policeman, a businessman, and two university graduates with doctoral degrees. Yet our collective skills, education, and professional experience couldn't help us at that moment. Without a solid rock for our anchor, we were left to the mercy of the current. Our credentials couldn't stop that current or tell us where we were on the ocean. They also did nothing to help our friend's wife who was with us; she was in the same predicament we were in. Furthermore, the other wives and families at home were absolutely panicked. They had no idea where we were, and they were up all night worrying about us. What if we were never found?

After being out all night in the darkness, we were finally rescued. Our families had contacted the equivalent of the Coast Guard in the Bahamas, and a strong military ship came and found us.

God has called you to be the anchor of your family. There are many treacherous influences in the world that attempt to swallow up you and your family; you are not strong enough to keep your family's "boat" secure if you as the anchor have nothing solid to hold on to. You need rock, not sand, or you will drift out of control and be overwhelmed. It's not just your own life, but also the lives of your family members, that depend on your anchor holding. If you can't hold, and if you get lost "at sea," what will they do? If men don't know where they're going, everyone gets lost because you bring your wives and children with you. However, when you are holding on to what is solid, they can trust in that and not fear.

> **Reconnect with and submit yourself to Jesus Christ as the Chief Cornerstone.**

Remember, Jesus said that you can't build your house on sand or your house will collapse. You can't say, "I'm a man. I have this, and I am that, so everything's going to be okay." That isn't enough. As heavy as an anchor is, it needs something heavier to enable it to hold steady. I'm a pastor, a businessman, a government advisor, an investor, a seminar facilitator and speaker, and an author, but when my storm comes, I have to grab onto a Rock that is mightier than I. King David wrote, *"From the ends of the earth I call to you, I call as my heart grows faint; lead me to the rock that is higher than I"* (Psalm 61:2). No matter how successful you are, you had better find the Rock because your family relies upon you for survival. Lock into Jesus, and secure your foundation. *"Christ Jesus himself* [is] *the chief cornerstone. In him the whole building is joined together and* rises to become a holy temple in the Lord" (Ephesians 2:20–21). In that one Stone, the whole building is held together.

When you have Jesus as your Cornerstone, God's Spirit lives within you as your "internal engine," and His power never fails. He will teach and strengthen you; He will guide your conscience and establish your convictions so you can reach shore safely. Just as our families called on a higher authority—the Coast Guard—to help us in our crisis, the Holy Spirit will direct and protect you in both the calm and stormy seas of your life. Even if there is darkness all around you, He will guide you in the right direction. Again, David wrote, *"If I say, 'Surely the darkness will hide me and the light become night around me,' even the darkness will not be dark to you; the night will shine like the day, for darkness is as light to you"* (Psalm 139:11–12).

Built to Handle the Future

I have worked with leaders who encountered crises in their lives and suddenly realized there was a void in their plans; they didn't know what to do because they had never prepared for it. It's not as important what happens to you as it is what you do about what happens. Think again of the construction workers digging the foundation for the hotel. They put so much concrete and steel into that hole that it reminded me of God's process of building men. I believe the contractor spent more time on the foundation than the building itself.

When God works on a foundation, He does the same thing. If you make Jesus your Cornerstone, God will build you so well that He will know you can handle the height of the building. He won't be concerned about you crumbling. If you don't know Christ as your personal Cornerstone, don't go another day without that assurance. I'm not talking about "religion" or "church." I'm talking about your reconnecting with and submitting yourself to Jesus Christ as the Chief Cornerstone. We have to submit to Him because, without Him, we are nothing and can do nothing. (See John 15:5.)

We've seen that an anchor is known by the storms it survives. What does this mean for you in practical terms? We don't want to think about certain scenarios, but what would you do, for example, if your wife died? Are you ready for that? Could you handle that storm? First, you would have to drop anchor fast and hang on to the Rock. Next, you would have to make sure you didn't move from that spot, because your children would be hanging on to you, looking to you to hold them together. You would have to stay on the Rock because temptation might come to prey on your weaknesses during your time of grief.

As you hold on to the Rock in the midst of whatever crisis you face, your foundation will remain sure. Then, as Paul said, you will be able to build a temple to God on it. *"In [Christ] the whole building is joined together and rises to become a holy temple in the Lord"* (Ephesians 2:21). If your building is pure, who dwells in it? God comes to dwell in a well-built life and a well-built family. If He's your Cornerstone, He lives in you. And if you are a strong foundation in Him, He lives in whatever you're holding together—whether it's a marriage, a family, a church, or a business. It becomes a holy dwelling place for Him.

A Man for All Seasons

Everyone who hears these words of mine and puts them into practice is like a wise man who built his house on the rock.

The rain came down, the streams rose, and the winds blew and beat against that house; yet it did not fall. But everyone who hears these words of mine and does not put them into practice is like a foolish man who built his house on sand. The rain came down, the streams rose, and the winds blew and beat against that house, and it fell with a great crash.

(Matthew 7:24–25)

Jesus said, *"The rain came."* He didn't say, "The rain *might* come." In other words, both the guy who builds on rock and the guy who builds on sand have to go through the storm.

One of my greatest mentors, Oral Roberts, taught me an important maxim: "Son, if you're going to be successful in life, expect the best and prepare for the worst." That advice has kept me sane. Expect the best—that's a good attitude. But prepare for the worst—that's a sane attitude. We go through various seasons in life, and we need to be prepared for them all by establishing our lives on the Rock.

A Scripture verse that helped establish me when I was a teenager still guides my life today. This verse is critical for spiritual and personal success: *"To every thing there is a season"* (Ecclesiastes 3:1 KJV). Everything in life has a season. That knowledge saved my life. This means that whatever difficulties we're experiencing are not going to last. However, it also means that whatever we are enjoying now will probably not last. Many of us do not want to hear this, and that is why we experience depression when we lose something—we think that everything is forever.

Let me suggest to you that even though you are in Christ Jesus, you are not immune to storms. We look at people who are men and women of God, who are faithful in service to

Him, who are praying people, who have given big seminars and conferences and crusades, who have built ministries, who have served people greatly, but who find themselves in crises, and we say, "This isn't supposed to happen to people like them." It doesn't matter what kind of "house" you have, the storm is coming. The issue is not really the storm. The issue is the foundation. I don't know what your storm is going to be. It might not be what your best friend's storm is, or what the person next to you in church is going through. But it is coming. I want you to be able to say, "I'm going through a tough one, but my anchor is holding. Last year I was prospering and this year I'm broke, but I still have my anchor. I'm holding on to Jesus. It's only a season." You have to keep on believing.

> **Both the guy who builds on rock and the guy who builds on sand have to go through the storm.**

"To every thing there is a season, and a time to every purpose under the heaven" (Ecclesiastes 3:1 KJV). You are not to trust in the permanence of anything on earth except for your relationship with God. Even your spouse is for a season. Parents, friends, coworkers, pastors, church members—they're all seasonal. Be prepared for the season of living without them. We must have our anchor on the Rock, because the Rock has no season—He is eternal. *"The eternal God is your refuge, and underneath are the everlasting arms"* (Deuteronomy 33:27). Even with those who tell you, "The Lord sent me to work with you," you can expect their departure at some point. Don't necessarily plan them into your future. This perspective has kept my blood pressure at a normal level. So

when a staff member comes to me and says, "The Lord told me it's time to move on," I say, "Well, praise God, thank you for your contribution the last twenty years. Now, what do you need to help you get where you're going?"

To everything there is a season. Suppose your business is going well. Prepare now for a time when your business might not go well; decide what you will do if your business goes through some tough times. Don't panic and say, "God has left me and the devil has taken over." No, that's just a season. Or maybe in the season you're going through, nothing is working. You have to shut the doors to your business and go back to a job. God is telling you, "That's okay. Go to the job." Why? "It's a seasonal job." Perhaps you don't like your current job. God says, "That's no problem; everything is seasonal." Think in those terms. You have to know how to handle what life brings you. You have to be an anchor that is not driven by every wind and wave.

> You have to know how to handle what life brings and not be driven by every wind and wave.

You have to be tough, men, because the season will change. If your baby died, or your wife had a miscarriage, or your business collapsed next month, what would you do? A young man may say, "I don't know what to do, man, she left me." Let the season go. Get on with your life, and fulfill your purpose. Be the man God created you to be. Let the message of God come into your spirit, and let His hammer come down and beat on the weak spots in your life, because you're a strong man with Christ as your Cornerstone. You can handle the tough times. Men, when the storm hits and you realize the whole ship is rocking and reeling, and you didn't expect it, your wife didn't expect it, the children didn't expect it, the church didn't expect it, and now you're looking at the vision, the destiny, and the dream, and saying, "What am I going to do?" God says, "You're the anchor—grab onto the Rock." Everybody else is hanging on to you, and in your fear, you have to hang on to the Rock. If you lose your grip on Him, the whole ship may sink.

Often, my friends and I have gone out on our boats to fish at six o'clock in the morning, and the water is like glass as we speed over the ocean. By one o'clock in the afternoon, however, a storm may be coming, and since we're out ten miles from shore, we have to start tying everything down. The season has changed, and the boat will rock during the storm, but everyone knows what to do; we've already been trained; we've prepared for the storm. We know to put the anchor down. We actually dive down and put that anchor under the rock personally. And then we brace everything. When the storm is upon us, it's too late to do anything else; the season has come. We're beaten about by the wind and waves, and after about fifteen or twenty minutes, it passes us by. It's peaceful again, and we can go back to fishing.

It will be the same with you. Once you have committed to the Rock and have prepared for the changing seasons of life, you will be able to ride out the storm and then go back to fishing. It's going to be all right, and it's going to be even better fishing because the storm will have stirred up more fish. Behind every broken experience is a wealthy experience. There is peace in the promise that nothing earthly lasts, but the Rock is eternal.

The Stone for the Storm

"But everyone who hears these words of mine and does not put them into practice is like a foolish man who built his house on sand" (Matthew 7:26). Jesus calls those who ignore His words foolish. You may be a CEO or have Ph.D., but you are a foolish CEO or Ph.D. if you have not anchored yourself to the Rock that does not move. Men, God did not make you to become fools. He made you to become wise.

Your family needs you. Your business needs you. Your community needs you. With Christ as your Cornerstone, you are a strong, interlocking foundation. *"See, I lay a stone in Zion, a chosen and precious cornerstone, and the one who trusts in him will never be put to shame"* (1 Peter 2:6). With Christ as your Cornerstone, it doesn't matter what happens because you are always winning. You will not be made ashamed. This is a promise. No matter what your ministry is going through, Jesus tells you to anchor yourself on the Rock, and you will not be disgraced. So when the waves crash, let them crash. You have the Stone for the storm.

What is the cornerstone of your family? What kind of foundation do you have? Will your anchor hold in the storms? You can be the father God purposed you to be. The coming chapters will teach you specific functions of true fatherhood that will enable you to be the foundation of your family as you rely on the Chief Cornerstone. Then you can teach your sons and other young men to be foundations in their generation.

CHAPTER PRINCIPLES

1. The male is the foundation, but the Chief Cornerstone is Jesus Christ.

2. Without the Cornerstone, the foundation falls apart.

3. If you make Jesus your Cornerstone, God will build you so well that you will be able to handle the height of the building.

4. An anchor is known by the storms it survives. As you hold on to the Rock in the midst of whatever crisis you face, your foundation will remain sure. God comes to dwell in a well-built life and a well-built family. *"In [Christ] the whole building is joined together and rises to become a holy temple in the Lord"* (Ephesians 2:21).

5. We go through various seasons in life, and we need to be prepared for them all by establishing our lives on the Rock.

6. Committed Christians are not immune to the storms of life.

7. Behind every broken experience is a wealthy experience.

8. With Christ as your Cornerstone, no matter what happens, you are always winning, and you will not be made ashamed. (See 1 Peter 2:6.)

Part 2

THE ROLE OF THE MALE:

Ten Basic Functions of Fatherhood

Chapter 4

FATHER AS SOURCE
AND PROGENITOR

The Functions of Fatherhood

The standard by which we should measure and train fathers can be found within these ten basic functions of true fatherhood:

1. Progenitor
2. Source
3. Sustainer and Nourisher
4. Protector
5. Teacher
6. Disciplinarian
7. Leader
8. Head
9. Caring One
10. Developer

In chapter one, we saw that the word *father* in the Bible is *ab* in the Old Testament and *pater* in the New Testament, and that these words denote "source" and "progenitor." God is the

Source of all substance and all life. He is the Progenitor who creates all things and then supports and upholds them. In this chapter, we will look at these vital functions more specifically and how they apply to us as earthly fathers.

God the Father as Source

God is Father by both nature and function. He is the Father of creation. God sent forth His Word and created all that is. *"All things were created by* [Christ Jesus, the Word of God]. *Without Him was not anything made that was made"* (John 1:3). (See also Genesis 1; Isaiah 63; Romans 1:20.) As the Source of all that is, God was "pregnant"—if I may use that analogy— with the seen and unseen world. He carried the seed of the universe. As the Source, God the Father had everything in Him before anything was. So God created the entire universe and brought into being all that is from nothing (*ex nihilo*). The Hebrew verb for creating is *bara*. The only proper subject for *bara* is God, for only He creates. That which produces or creates is the source—the father.

God the Father as Progenitor

Remember that a progenitor is one who upholds and supports the coming generations. God *is* Life. He created human beings and gave them the ability to reproduce and pass along life to their children.

The highest honor God can give a man is to designate him a father. "Father" is His own title. If He conveys this title upon the man, then it must be the highest designation and honor that any human being can have. In fact, fatherhood is the ultimate work of the male-man. Fatherhood is a heavy honor and a tremendous responsibility. The father's job is to uphold and support the generation he brings forth.

Humanity's Identity

God created human beings with genes, which are the source and substance of life. These genes are passed down from parent to child. Our genes determine physical characteristics, behaviors, emotional reactions, and instincts, as well as how we process our thoughts. At the core of our natural identities are our genes. When a man sows seed into the receptor (the woman) and a child is conceived, the next generation is given its identity by the genes.

Adam was the father of the human race. His genes were released into humanity. As the progenitor of humanity, what identity did humanity inherit from Adam? Although God gave him life to pass along, Adam rebelled and rejected His life-giving Creator, and therefore death was passed on in Adam's seed.

> *Therefore, just as sin entered the world through one man, and death through sin, and in this way death came to all men, because all sinned....* (Romans 5:12)

Because Adam allowed sin to enter the world, his descendents were born with a sinful nature and with bodies that would eventually die. His son Cain even became a murderer. The inheritance we received from Adam was death—both spiritual and physical death. Since we are all Adam's offspring, we need to change fathers as soon as possible. We need to be rebirthed with everlasting seed and genes by the heavenly Father, through His Son Jesus Christ. This gives us spiritual life and the promise of physical resurrection in the future.

Note that in the garden of Eden, when Eve gave in to the temptation of Satan, nothing apparently happened. She picked the fruit, and nothing happened. She bit into the fruit, and nothing happened. She swallowed the fruit, and nothing happened. But then she took the fruit to Adam—her husband and "father." When he ate the fruit, this is the very next thing that happened:

> *Then the eyes of both of them were opened, and they realized they were naked; so they sewed fig leaves together and made coverings for themselves. Then the man and his wife heard the sound of the LORD God as he was walking in the garden in the cool of the day, and they hid from the LORD God among the trees of the garden. But the LORD God called to the man, "Where are you?" He answered, "I heard you in the garden, and I was afraid because I was naked; so I hid."*
> (Genesis 3:7–10)

When Adam disobeyed God, something went wrong. All hell broke loose. Human beings experienced shame, fear, and separation from God. When the man ate the fruit, in his act of separating from the Father, all his children were contaminated—including his first "offspring," Eve.

Exodus 20:5 reveals, *"You shall not bow down to* [idols] *or worship them; for I, the LORD your God, am a jealous God, punishing the children for the sin of the fathers to the third and fourth generation of those who hate me."* Women are not identified as the ones who transfer sin; men are. So the only way to get rid of Adam's seed of sin is to renounce him—and his stepfather, the devil—as your father. You have to renounce the generations of sin that have begotten you. Only the Second Adam, Jesus, can birth new life in you and break the curse of sin and death that you inherited from your original father, Adam.

Adam did what many men still do today; he blamed Eve for his sin. (See Genesis 3:11–12.) Men are still blaming the women and mothers in our cultures for the social problems we're having with our children. The truth is that the root problem is the fathers.

Men, stop blaming women. Yes, Eve was *"deceived"* (1 Timothy 2:14), but Adam sinned, rejected his Father, and, through his seed, became the progenitor of sin to all forthcoming generations. The fall of man was the result of a father receiving instructions from his "offspring," instead of the other way around; the resource gave to the source what had not come from the Father.

Adam, as progenitor, sowed his seed of rebellion against the Father into all human generations, but Christ, as the Son of Man and the Everlasting Father, sowed God's seed of life into all who would be born again. Renounce the father of all lies and return to the Father of light and life.

Identity Comes from a Father

The greatest challenge for men today, especially young men, is that they suffer from an identity crisis. They lack the nurturing influence of a true father to give them identity. An identity doesn't come from a gang or the government or books. It comes from a father.

The only one who can give you your true identity as a man is a father. This fundamental principle is lacking in many of our cultures, and its absence is the source of many social problems. Most young men are running around looking for a father, and they can't find him. They're running to their friends but to no avail. You can't find fatherhood in another peer who is also looking for a father. You can't discover who you are by looking to someone who doesn't know who he or she is.

A man needs to be affirmed by a father in order to confirm his manhood. This is why so many young men yearn to hear their fathers say to them, "I love you, Son. You're a man now." Do you know why being Jewish carries such a strong identity? Jewish tradition, particularly in family relationships, has a very real sense of the "father spirit." This is rooted in a ceremony called bar mitzvah, in which a thirteen-year-old boy goes before the men and performs some prescribed traditional rites, after which the men say to him, "Now you are a man." From that day forward, that boy takes on a different spirit, for he is now a man. That's why Jewish communities are knitted so closely together and are so strong in business, tradition, and culture.

> The measure of a man's success is directly related to his effectiveness as a godly father.

Jewish fathers tell and show their boys what it means to have the identity of a man. This cultural practice is embedded in their history and can be traced back to biblical roots. This practice can also be found in many African and Eastern cultures where manhood is bestowed through a ritual.

Now pay close attention: If you haven't found your earthly father yet, God qualifies as your Father. Hallelujah! You can come to God and say, "God, what am I?" and He'll tell you, "You're My son." You must get your identity from Him.

> *But as many as received* [Jesus Christ], *to them gave he power to become the sons of God, even to them that believe on his name.* (John 1:12)

Second, God the Father will say to you, "Now mature into the image of My dear Son, Jesus Christ, and you will grow up in Him until you are a true man." Jesus the Son, who is also Everlasting Father, tells you, "You are a father." He gives you your identity as a father.

The principle of fatherhood, therefore, is simple: *You provide identity.*

A male can do nothing greater than fathering. He can earn a million dollars, but if he fails to fulfill God's calling upon him to father as God fathers, then he is a failure. He can own a huge home, have tremendous real estate holdings, manage a large stock portfolio, and have a billion-dollar estate, but if he neglects to father his family, he has failed.

A male who is physically strong but weak as a father is not a man. A male rich in possessions but poor in fathering is not a man. A male eloquent in words but silent as a father in teaching his household the Word and precepts of God is not a man. The measure of a man's success is directly related to his effectiveness as a godly father, for which God is the only true example and standard.

The Source of Sin Is Fatherlessness

At the root of sin is the absence of real fathers in our world. The sin problem is a fatherhood problem, because sin is the result of a man—Adam—who declared independence from God, his Source and Father. Adam believed he didn't need a father and that he could be a father without the Father. That is when the human race fell into rebellion against God.

One of the root meanings of the word *sin* in the New Testament, *hamartia*, is "separation." Adam separated himself from his Father and fell into a state of separation and sin. In other words, man could be called a "fatherless child" because of his own choice. Imagine that. Orphaned by choice! Homeless by choice! Separated from his Father by choice! How tragic was the choice of Adam to reject his Father.

> The only person in history who could father us was One who knew the Father—Jesus.

Adam became a fatherless child, yet Adam himself had children whom he inflicted with fatherlessness. And Adam's first "child" was not Cain. The first "offspring" that came out of Adam was a female. (See Genesis 2:20-24.) Since Adam spiritually orphaned himself, Eve and every subsequent offspring were spiritual orphans.

Recall that God had breathed life into Adam. *"The Lord God formed the man from the dust of the ground and breathed into his nostrils the breath of life, and the man became a living being"* (Genesis 2:7). But Adam cut himself off from God, his Father— the Source of his creation and life. Again, once Adam became fatherless, all he could pass on to his children was death.

A father can create or generate in his children only what he has received from his father. Father is the source, the creator, the generator, and the progenitor. Future generations can receive only what the father gives them. Since Adam rejected his Father, the only inheritance he had to give to future generations was sin and death—a fatherless inheritance.

One more point needs to be made here. All too often, women are lost and making many mistakes because their husbands do not understand the full ramifications of fatherhood as God intended. What they need is a man who can teach them about *the* Father, God. Without fathers, there is a curse upon women and future generations.

Turning the Hearts of the Children to Their Fathers

How can true fatherhood be restored? Salvation is the result of a Man—Jesus, the Second Adam—providing the orphaned children of humanity with the way to return to their Father and their original identity in Him. Remember, Adam voluntarily left his Father. The mission of Jesus was to return orphaned humanity back to God, and to restore earthly family relationships to the way He intended them to be. Malachi prophesied that this would begin to happen when John the Baptist prepared the way for the Messiah: *"He will turn the hearts of the fathers to their children, and the hearts of the children to their fathers; or else I will come and strike the land with a curse"* (Malachi 4:6). When the angel appeared to Zechariah, John the Baptist's father, telling him what would be the nature of his son's birth, he quoted those very words:

> *Many of the people of Israel will he bring back to the Lord their God. And he will go on before the Lord, in the spirit and power of Elijah,* **to turn the hearts of the fathers to their children** *and the disobedient to the wisdom of the*

righteous—to make ready a people prepared for the Lord.
(Luke 1:16-17, emphasis added)

The people needed to return to God the Father. John the Baptist was preparing them for what they desperately needed—One who could lead them back to their heavenly Father.

Jesus came to fix man's problem of fatherlessness. Many fathers are estranged from their children. Many homes are without fathers. Before Christ, Adam's children throughout the ages knew little about the Father because they were born fatherless as a result of Adam's sin and rejection of Him. The problem of fatherlessness that started with Adam still affects us to this day. Brothers, our nations could be healed right now if every man became a responsible father. The ten functions of fatherhood outlined at the beginning of this chapter will certainly help point us to what it means to be like our heavenly Father.

Men and women alike are looking for a father. Without God the Father, a husband does not know how to be a father to his wife or children. Without a father in the home, women end up babysitting their husbands. They take care of the man who is supposed to be their "father."

Jesus knew the Father and became the Source and Progenitor of a new race of fathers—those who know their heavenly Father through His Son. You cannot be a true father unless you have one yourself. The only person in history who could father us was One who knew the Father, and that person was Jesus.

Remember the example Jesus showed us even when He was dying on the cross. He took the time—as well as a few of his last fleeting breaths—to be a father to His mother. He gave instructions as the head, the oldest son in His family, since His earthly father, Joseph, was apparently dead. *"When Jesus saw his mother there, and the disciple whom he loved standing nearby, he said to his mother, 'Dear woman, here is your son,' and to the disciple, 'Here is your mother'"* (John 19:26–27). With those statements, Jesus put the responsibility of caring for his mother, Mary, in John's hands.

If you are the son in a home where your father has left or died, then you are the father of your mother, your sisters, and your household. Why? Because God has called men to be fathers like Him in order to turn the hearts of the children back to their Father God. If you understand this principle and responsibility and begin to apply it in your life, then God will answer your prayers for provision because He will father you as you also father your family.

Jesus and His Father

The greatest example of the critical role of father was demonstrated in the life of Jesus. He spoke of His Father more than anyone else. He expressed and emphatically confessed His need, dependency, and submission to His Father at every opportunity. He never hesitated to give credit to His Father for any activity or success, thereby confirming the sustaining work of God in His life. He saw His Father as the Source, Resource, and Purpose for His entire life.

Whenever He was questioned about His identity, His work, His purpose, His heritage, His power, His authority, His family, His message, His philosophy, His theology, His legitimacy, or His destiny, He referred to "My Father."

How many men do you know today who speak of their fathers in such a way? How many could and do give their fathers credit for most of their activities and successes? On the contrary, most men today consider it "less manly" to give credit to another because it is perceived as a weakness. What a stark contrast to the attitude of the ultimate Man, Jesus Christ! His perception and relationship with His Father should serve as the standard by which we measure the effectiveness and success of true fatherhood. In essence, the level at which your child refers to you is the measure of your effectiveness as a father. Consider these words of and about Jesus:

> Then they asked him, "Where is your father?" "You do not know me or my Father," Jesus replied. "If you knew me, you would know my Father also." (John 8:19)

> "I have much to say in judgment of you. But he who sent me is reliable, and what I have heard from him I tell the world." They did not understand that he was telling them about his Father. So Jesus said, "When you have lifted up the Son of Man, then you will know that I am the one I claim to be and that I do nothing on my own but speak just what the Father has taught me. The one who sent me is with me; he has not left me alone, for I always do what pleases him." (John 8:26–29)

> I am telling you what I have seen in the Father's presence, and you do what you have heard from your father.
> (John 8:38)

> "I am not possessed by a demon," said Jesus, "but I honor my Father and you dishonor me." (John 8:49)

> Jesus replied, "If I glorify myself, my glory means nothing. My Father, whom you claim as your God, is the one who glorifies me. Though you do not know him, I know him. If I said I did not, I would be a liar like you, but I do know him and keep his word." (John 8:54–55)

Jesus answered, "I did tell you, but you do not believe. The miracles I do in my Father's name speak for me."

(John 10:25)

My Father, who has given them to me, is greater than all; no one can snatch them out of my Father's hand. I and the Father are one. (John 10:29–30)

Do not believe me unless I do what my Father does. But if I do it, even though you do not believe me, believe the miracles, that you may know and understand that the Father is in me, and I in the Father. (John 10:37–38)

Jesus knew that the Father had put all things under his power, and that he had come from God and was returning to God. (John 13:3)

Philip said, "Lord, show us the Father and that will be enough for us." Jesus answered: "Don't you know me, Philip, even after I have been among you such a long time? Anyone who has seen me has seen the Father. How can you say, 'Show us the Father'? Don't you believe that I am in the Father, and that the Father is in me? The words I say to you are not just my own. Rather, it is the Father, living in me, who is doing his work. Believe me when I say that I am in the Father and the Father is in me; or at least believe on the evidence of the miracles themselves."

(John 14:8–11)

On that day you will realize that I am in my Father, and you are in me, and I am in you. Whoever has my commands and obeys them, he is the one who loves me. He who loves me will be loved by my Father, and I too will love him and show myself to him. (John 14:20–21)

I am the true vine, and my Father is the gardener.

(John 15:1)

This is to my Father's glory, that you bear much fruit, showing yourselves to be my disciples. As the Father has loved me, so have I loved you. Now remain in my love. If you obey my commands, you will remain in my love, just as I have obeyed my Father's commands and remain in his love.

(John 15:8–10)

I no longer call you servants, because a servant does not know his master's business. Instead, I have called you friends, for everything that I learned from my Father I have made known to you. (John 15:15)

Though I have been speaking figuratively, a time is coming when I will no longer use this kind of language but will tell you plainly about my Father. (John 16:25)

I came from the Father and entered the world; now I am leaving the world and going back to the Father. (John 16:28)

After Jesus said this, he looked toward heaven and prayed: "Father, the time has come. Glorify your Son, that your Son may glorify you." (John 17:1)

Now this is eternal life: that they may know you, the only true God, and Jesus Christ, whom you have sent. I have brought you glory on earth by completing the work you gave me to do. And now, Father, glorify me in your presence with the glory I had with you before the world began. (John 17:3–5)

Righteous Father, though the world does not know you, I know you, and they know that you have sent me.

(John 17:25)

Jesus said, "Do not hold on to me, for I have not yet returned to the Father. Go instead to my brothers and tell them, 'I am returning to my Father and your Father, to my God and your God.'" (John 20:17)

Again Jesus said, "Peace be with you! As the Father has sent me, I am sending you." (John 20:21)

Jesus declared, *"If God were your Father, you would love me, for I came from God and now am here. I have not come on my own but he sent me"* (John 8:42). Jesus was addressing those who did not believe in Him. The root of their unbelief was not knowing the Father. If you don't know the Father, you cannot know His Son. Unbelief is caused by fatherlessness.

Similarly, wayward children, in effect, have no father. They have no respect for their elders and cannot submit to authority. Children need to learn about God the Father through fathers who teach them about Him and His ways.

> **Fathers are progenitors. They create in their children what their fathers created in them.**

I thank God for my earthly father. He made certain that his children respected their elders. He taught me about authority. My father generated in me a knowledge of what submission, authority, and respect are all about. He was the source of my understanding about fathers because he knew God the Father.

Unfortunately, many children today do not have a father in the home. They don't have the benefit of a father to create within them the honor and respect they need for other authority figures. Instead, they curse people on the streets, talk back to their teachers, and utterly disrespect their elders.

Without godly fathers creating in us a knowledge, respect, and fear of God, we are destined to be spiritual orphans. By not knowing our real Father—and not having our identity in Him—we inevitably substitute a fraud and counterfeit. Speaking to the religious leaders of His day who rebelled against His teaching and questioned His identity, integrity, and legitimacy, Jesus said,

> *You belong to your father, the devil, and you want to carry out your father's desire. He was a murderer from the beginning, not holding to the truth, for there is no truth in him. When he lies, he speaks his native language, for he is a liar and the father of lies.* (John 8:44)

Remember, fathers are progenitors. They create in their children what their fathers created in them. They birth generations after them that are like themselves and their forefathers. If they are without their heavenly Father, their counterfeit father is the devil; therefore, they create generations that are like Satan instead of like Father God. Satan is a "stepfather" who claimed rights to the children of men when they rebelled against their loving Father.

If you have the wrong father, you'll grow up with the wrong "genes." A man with a countefeit father will birth defective children. How are they defective? They are filled with what has been generated in them—sin, lies, and murderous hate.

A New Father and Identity

Because the male is noted in Scripture as being the source and progenitor of generations, it was to Abraham, not Sarah, that God said, *"I will establish my covenant as an everlasting covenant between me and you* [Abraham] *and your descendants after you for the generations to come, to be your God and the God of your descendants after you"* (Genesis 17:7). God established a covenant relationship between Himself and Abraham, and Abraham and his descendents consequently had an identity that was fully connected to God. God did not indicate that Sarah was a progenitor, but He also promised her by saying, *"I will bless her and will surely give you a son by her. I will bless her so that she will be the mother of nations; kings of peoples will come from her"* (Genesis 17:16). Only the man's seed can generate the conception of generations. Only the male has generating, creative power. He is the source, and the wife is the incubator.

Jesus knew that the Jews of His day had become fatherless in regard to their relationship with God. They thought that Abraham was their father, failing to recognize that the God and Father of Abraham was their Source. They had lost a sense of their true identity. The Jews did not start as a race of people with father Abraham. It was God, Abraham's Father, who called them into being. Like the Jews, we need to change fathers. We have lost our original Father God, and we follow a stepfather, the devil, with contaminated blood and genes filled with evil and ignorance.

Jesus wanted God's rebellious children to turn their hearts back to the Father and away from Satan. Everything He did was to get us back to the Father. Again, after His resurrection, Jesus said, *"I am returning to my Father and your Father, to my God and your God"* (John 20:17). He is saying to us, "I have paid the price; I have shed My blood. I have descended into Hades, taken the keys, unlocked the door, and set the captives free. I have risen from the dead. My work is finished. I have created a new generation of children birthed by My Father, who is now your Father God. I am going to My Father and yours so He can be fully your Father again." He sent the Holy Spirit to live within those who had been restored to their relationship with the Father.

Jesus asserted that we must be born of water and the Holy Spirit. (See John 3:5.) Why? Through faith in Jesus, God has provided a way for us to be set free from our stepfather and born anew into His family, with Him as our Father. Paul wrote that we are "new creations" in Christ Jesus. (See 2 Corinthians 5:17.) That new creation includes a new Father and a new identity.

> **God has provided a way for us to be born anew into His family, with Him as our Father.**

"For to us a child is born, to us a son is given, and the government will be on his shoulders. And he will he called Wonderful Counselor, Mighty God, Everlasting Father, Prince of Peace" (Isaiah 9:6). Jesus came to us as a Son, a child of His Father, to show us how a child of God the Father should look, talk, and act. He asserted, *"I do nothing on my own but speak just what the Father has taught me. The one who sent me is with me; he has not left me alone, for I always do what pleases him"* (John 8:28–29). Whoever saw Jesus also saw the Father. (See John 14:9–11.) In Jesus, we learn what a child of the Father is like, as well as what the Father is like.

Since Jesus is the Everlasting Father as well as the Son, His fatherhood requires us to be submitted and obedient to His every Word, because all that He says and commands comes straight from the Father. In this way, we are transformed by the Holy Spirit into the likeness of Jesus Christ. (See 2 Corinthians 3:18.) In His likeness is the perfect image of what it means to be both a child of the heavenly Father and a father to our own offspring, so that their hearts will be turned to the Father.

Remember these key principles for knowing God the Father:

- As the Source, God the Father had everything in Him before anything was. Everything that exists was in God.
- God is the Progenitor. He upholds and supports all that He created.
- Sin is the result of the first man—Adam—turning his back on his Father.
- Salvation is the result of a Man—Jesus, the Second Adam—providing us with the way to return to the Father.
- Jesus knew the Father and became the Source and Progenitor of a new race of fathers who know the Father through the Son.
- Fathers are progenitors. They birth generations after them that are like themselves and their forefathers. When a man is fathered by God, he produces godly fathers.
- Fathers are the source of instruction, information, and knowledge about God the Source.
- We learn how God disciplines, teaches, instructs, and acts through an earthly father who embodies the Father.

Because fathers are the source, they must sustain, nourish, and protect all that comes out of them. That is our next topic as we understand the functions of fatherhood. In the next chapter, we will come to understand more fully how God, as the Source and Progenitor, is also the Sustainer, Nourisher, and Protector. As the Source and Progenitor, God sustains all that He fathers or creates. He alone can bring something into existence, and He alone can maintain it.

CHAPTER PRINCIPLES

1. "Father" is the highest honor God bestows on men.

2. The principle of fatherhood is that fathers provide identity.

3. The measure of a man's success is directly related to his effectiveness as a godly father, for which God is the ultimate standard and only true example.

4. The source of sin is fatherlessness.

5. Jesus came to fix man's problem of fatherlessness. Salvation is the result of Jesus, the Second Adam, providing us with the way to return to the Father and our original identity in Him.

6. God has called men to be fathers like He is, in order to turn the hearts of the children back to the Father. If you understand this principle and responsibility and begin to apply it in your life, then God will answer your prayers for provision because He will father you as you also father your family.

7. The level at which your child refers to you is the measure of your effectiveness as a father.

8. Fathers are progenitors—the source that generates, supports, and upholds the coming generations.

Chapter 5

FATHER AS SUSTAINER, NURTURER, AND PROTECTOR

E verything we know about fatherhood begins in Genesis—the book of beginnings. Consider this process of creation: God is the self-sustaining One. He doesn't use anything from any other source to create. He *is* the Source. Before creation, *Elohim*, the name for God that reflects His triune nature, decided to bring humanity into existence. *"For he chose us in him before the creation of the world to be holy and blameless in his sight. In love…"* (Ephesians 1:4). God was "pregnant" with us before He created the universe. He decided to have sons, offspring, spirit children who would be made in His image and likeness.

In His purpose, foreknowledge, and predestination—in His supernatural womb—*Elohim* created His children. His plan for us was not only that we be created in His image, but also that we exercise authority and dominion, just as He does. Since there was nothing for His children to rule over, God spoke the universe into being. Creation is the product of God's purpose for His children. He spoke creation into being in order to sustain those made in His image.

I believe that God created millions upon millions of galaxies, stars, and planets in order to sustain the balance of the universe. This vast universe baffles scientists. The more they discover about it, the more they realize how little they know. The universe is bigger and greater than they ever imagined. Some say it is expanding. The truth is that it is infinitely greater than anything they can imagine because the infinite God created it for the man into whom He would breathe infinite, eternal life.

God Created Everything to Sustain Man

At the center of the universe's purpose is humanity. David declared,

When I consider your heavens, the work of your fingers, the moon and the stars, which you have set in place, what is man that you [God] are mindful of him, the son of man that you care for him? You made him a little lower than the heavenly beings and crowned him with glory and honor. You made him ruler over the works of your hands; you put everything under his feet.   (Psalm 8:3–6)

The whole universe was created just for God's children to have a place to exercise the Father's dominion, and for their nature (image and likeness) to manifest the Father's.

God created all that is, and thus became the Source, the *Ab*, the Father of creation. What is a father? One who produces something and then sustains it. Out of God the Father came the Word, His Son, who spoke all things into being:

In the beginning was the Word, and the Word was with God, and the Word was God. He was with God in the beginning.

Through him all things were made; without him nothing was made that has been made. In him was life, and that life was the light of men. (John 1:1–4)

Not only did the Word create all that is, but the Word also upholds, supports, and sustains everything created:

But in these last days he has spoken to us by his Son, whom he appointed heir of all things, and through whom he made the universe. The Son is the radiance of God's glory and the exact representation of his being, sustaining all things by his powerful word. (Hebrews 1:2–3)

Out of the Father came the Son. He is the eternal and only begotten Son of the Father; He *is* God.

For to which of the angels did God ever say, "You are my Son; today I have become your Father"? Or again, "I will be his Father, and he will be my Son"? And again, when God brings his firstborn into the world, he says, "Let all God's angels worship him." (Hebrews 1:5–6)

The Son, as the Word, spoke all creation into being, which would sustain humanity. The Father always sustains what He produces.

Now we have set the stage for Adam. In eternity, before time and creation, all humanity had been conceived in the mind of God. God first created all things in order to sustain humanity, whom He would create in His image. Then, because He wanted everybody to have one source (father), He finished everyone and put the initial seed for their existence in one body—Adam's.

For eternity, the male is the father of human society and social relationships. He is the source of the human family. This puts an awesome reponsibility on him. The male, as a father, is the source, sustainer, nurturer, and protector of the woman, because God took the woman out of the man.

In our society, too many women are called upon to do a father's job. Women were not created to be the sustainer. Too many men have abandoned their women and left them alone to sustain themselves and the offspring that the men gave them. Whatever is produced by a father must be sustained and nourished by him.

God did not go back to the soil to produce a woman. Why? He did not want the soil to support the woman. God made Adam to be a father. God wanted a father to represent Him on earth. Out of a father—Adam—was produced a woman to be fathered, sustained, and nurtured by the man. So God created man to be a father like Himself. Together, the man and the woman come together in marriage. From the beginning God said, *"For this reason a man will leave his father and mother and be united to his wife, and they will become one flesh"* (Genesis 2:24). Notice again that the Scripture never said that the wife leaves her father. Why? Because her husband is to be her father, her source, and her sustainer.

> The church cannot fix society's problems when the foundation is out of place.

Out of man came the woman and marriage. Out of marriage came children. So then we have a family. When families gather together, we have a community. When a multiplicity of communities come together, we have a society and a nation.

Men as Sustainers Are Society's Foundation

I want you to picture the problem with our societies and nations, as well as the solution. God created man, and out of him was produced a woman. That means Adam, as her source, was responsible for nourishing and sustaining her.

If societies and nations have problems with drugs, unwed mothers, teenage pregnancy, corruption, violence, and the like, then they must go back to the foundation in order to solve the problem. If they have a national problem, then they must go back into the communities to find the problem. Obviously, the community's problems affect the nation, which is a multiplicity of communities. Community problems are rooted in the families that make up each community. When we check to see what the families' problems are, we must look at marriages. When we examine the condition of our marriages, we discover that husbands and wives are divorced, mothers have been abandoned, and men are not sustaining their families. What does all this boil down to? Brothers, we are at the root of the problem affecting the nations! The foundational source has a problem: men are not being the fathers God created them to be.

Understand this: The church cannot fix society's problems when the foundation is out of place. *"When the foundations are being destroyed, what can the righteous do?"* (Psalm 11:3). No matter how much the church works at correcting social ills, if the foundation that God laid for the family is not in place, even the work of the righteous will not be successful. The devil does not care as much if the church is filled with women, because as long as men do not come back to their heavenly Father, then the women and their children are fatherless.

Godly fatherhood is the foundation of the family, the church, and the culture.

The primary mission of the church is to be fishers of men. (See Matthew 4:19; Mark 1:17.) The church calls men back to their original Father, and they are restored to the Father by salvation through the Son. When men return to the Father, they can be sustained and nurtured by their Source and then become the sustainers they are called to be for their families. Remember, when humanity fell, God never asked the woman where she was, but the man. *"The LORD God called to the man, 'Where are you?'"* (Genesis 3:9).

> A nation can be sustained, nurtured, and protected only when men are fathers like the heavenly Father.

In other words, Adam was out of position. The foundation had been shaken and destroyed. The whole of creation was unbalanced. God had fathered Adam so that he could father and sustain Eve. Without fathers, the marriage, the family, the community, and the nation lie in shambles. A nation can be sustained, nurtured, and protected only when men are fathers like the Father.

Isaiah prophesied what would happen when men abandoned fatherhood and the foundations of the culture shattered. *"Youths oppress my people, women rule over them. O my people, your guides lead you astray; they turn you from the path"* (Isaiah 3:12). When women rule exclusively, the whole nation, community, or household is in trouble.

Isaiah 3:12 describes a society or nation much like those in the world today in which women chase after men, men rule like mad children, and boys—not men—become leaders. Isaiah prophesied that there will be a scarcity of real men who are like God the Father. In such cultures, immorality and satanic oppression will be rampant; men will become like women (receivers) and indulge in homosexuality. When such immorality sets in, women will rule men, and men will become like children. They will become feminized, responding to life like women.

Woman, when a man wants to marry you, do not ask him if he loves you; ask him who he loves. If his love for God is not his first priority, then he is a poor prospect for a fulfilling, lasting relationship. Refuse to form relationships with plastic men who melt when the heat and pressures of life get turned up high. Find someone who is real. Until you find a man who knows that God the Father is his Source and Sustainer, you must lean on Jesus. He will husband you until you find a man who can be a godly husband and father.

If an enemy wanted to destroy a nation, a community, or a family, whom would the enemy attack? The father is a primary target of Satan's attack! When fathers move out of their place as sustainers, nurturers, and protectors, the foundations are destroyed and society crumbles.

Faithful to Sustain His Offspring

As I travel around the world, I see evil everywhere. At times, I ask the same question Jeremiah did: *"Why does the way of the wicked prosper?"* (Jeremiah 12:1). There are drug pushers, pimps, thieves, and dishonest businesspeople everywhere who have big homes, nice cars, boats, and lots of money. What is the ultimate source of all that they have? How do they sustain their lives? The answer to those questions is the same as the answer to the question of why the righteous prosper. The

Father (Sustainer) sends the rain upon the just and the unjust because everyone and everything is from Him. (See Matthew 5:45.) If something comes from you as a *pater* (father), then you must sustain it, even though it is rotten, no good, horrible, and rebellious. Why? Because God is a good, faithful, and patient Father! He sustains, nourishes, and protects. He *"is patient with you, not wanting anyone to perish, but everyone to come to repentance"* (2 Peter 3:9).

Jesus understood that with God as His continual Source, only good things could come from Him. The religious leaders criticized Jesus for doing miracles, saying that He was from the devil. Yet He answered His critics by saying,

> *Which of you fathers, if your son asks for a fish, will give him a snake instead? Or if he asks for an egg, will give him a scorpion? If you then, though you are evil, know how to give good gifts to your children, how much more will your Father in heaven give the Holy Spirit to those who ask him!* (Luke 11:11-13)

What has Jesus taught us? Simply this: God's sustenance does not depend on behavior or how it is received. He sustains what He creates because of His goodness. Similarly, an earthly father who is modeling the heavenly Father will sustain, nourish, and protect that which comes out of him as the source.

Remember the parable of the prodigal son (more aptly called the parable of the loving father)? The ambitious and ungrateful son took his good inheritance, left home, squandered the inheritance, and ended up living in a pigpen. When this lost son returned home, however, the father still loved him. Not only was he willing to sustain him, but he also threw him a party to celebrate his homecoming.

If you stay away from God, He will sustain you even with pig slop, if that's what you want. Why? You are still the son, and He is still the faithful Father. His faithfulness doesn't change just because you sin or rebel. God says, "I'll feed you slop if that's what you want to eat. The pigs and the garbage they eat are mine, and I will give them to you."

When the lost son came to himself, he said, *"How many of my father's hired men have food to spare, and here I am starving to death! I will set out and go back to my father"* (Luke 15:17–18). He realized that the food in his father's house was better than the food in the pigpen. You can decide upon the quality of life you want to live, just as the lost son did. God will feed you whatever you want to "eat." If you hang out with the pigs, you will eat pig slop. If you return home to your Father, you can live in the fullness of His grace and provision. The choice is yours.

> **Though tempted, Spirit-filled believers have the strength from the Father to overcome the enemy.**

Sustained to Withstand Evil

As men return to their Father, they must realize that He is able to sustain them in trials and temptations as they seek to live according to His example of fatherhood. Paul wrote that *"all things were created by [Jesus] and for Him. He is before all things, and in him all things hold together"* (Colossians 1:16–17). God sustains all that He created through Jesus, the Word. Even the devil could not exist without His permission. God does not tempt you, but He does allow Satan to tempt you, as we saw in a previous chapter. But you have God's promise that no temptation or trial comes your way that you cannot withstand. He will sustain you spiritually in the midst of that temptation: *"No temptation has seized you except what is common to man. And God is faithful; he will not let you be tempted beyond what you can bear. But when you are tempted, he will also provide a way out so that you can stand up under it"* (1 Corinthians 10:13).

No demon can come into your presence without permission from the Father. Though tempted, Spirit-filled believers have the strength from the Father to overcome the enemy. The next time any temptation comes your way, remember that it comes by permission. In it, there will be something for you to learn, and a way will be provided by the Father for you to overcome.

> *Consider it pure joy, my brothers, whenever you face trials of many kinds, because you know that the testing of your faith develops perseverance. Perseverance must finish its work so that you may be mature and complete, not lacking anything.* (James 1:2–4)

> *In this you greatly rejoice, though now for a little while you may have had to suffer grief in all kinds of trials. These have come so that your faith—of greater worth than gold, which perishes even though refined by fire—may be proved genuine and may result in praise, glory and honor when Jesus Christ is revealed.* (1 Peter 1:6–7)

Through trials and tests, you will grow and come to understand more fully how God is the Source and Sustainer for everything you face in life.

An Unshakable Foundation

The Source and Sustainer of every man is Christ. It is time for churches to go after men and lead them back to the Father through Jesus Christ. When men get back to Christ, they return to their rightful position in creation as fathers like the Father. Only then can men bring healing to the brokenness and sustain their marriages, families, communities, and nations.

Men who live like the heavenly Father are the unshakable foundation God purposed from the beginning by fathering Adam. In Christ, men return to their Source—God the Father— and then become sustainers, nurturers, and protectors.

The function of fathering like the Father who sustains, nurtures, and protects encompasses these principles:

- Creation is the product of God's purpose for His children. In His foreknowledge, God spoke creation into being in order to sustain those created in His image.

- God wanted everyone to have one source, so He put the initial seed for their existence in one body—Adam's.

- The foundation for the whole human family is the male. Everything to sustain women should come from their fathers or their husbands (who are also their "fathers").

- A father, like God, sustains, nourishes, and protects what comes out of him as the source.

- Fatherhood is the foundation of the family, the church, and the culture.

Now we will explore how a father supports and raises up future generations in godliness and righteousness by fulfilling his function as teacher.

CHAPTER PRINCIPLES

1. God created man to be a father like Himself in order to represent Him on earth and to sustain that which comes out of him.

2. Out of man came the woman and marriage. Out of marriage came children and a family. Families create communities, and communities create societies or nations. Therefore, fathers are the foundation of all societies.

3. The church cannot fix society's problems when the foundation is out of place.

4. A father, like God, sustains, nourishes, and protects that which comes out of him as the source—regardless of behavior or how his provision is received.

5. Men who are fathers like the Father are the unshakable foundation God purposed from the beginning when He created Adam.

Chapter 6

FATHER AS TEACHER

Whatever we find in the first two chapters of Genesis is verified throughout Scripture and lays a foundation for understanding fatherhood, marriage, family, and culture. God gave Adam the information that needed to be taught. Essentially, God the Father teaches each father so that he can teach his wife, children, and upcoming generations.

The Father Receives the Instructions

It is important to remember that the biblical record in Genesis gives no evidence that Eve received the instructions concerning the garden or the Tree of Knowledge of Good and Evil directly from God; only Adam received direct instructions from Him. (See Genesis 2:15-17.) God the Father, therefore, made Adam responsible for teaching the woman and everyone else who came after him what He had said. This pattern is repeated with each new family.

This is clearly seen in God's interactions with Abraham. God told him,

Shall I hide from Abraham what I am about to do? Abraham will surely become a great and powerful nation, and all nations on earth will be blessed through him. For I have

chosen him, so that he will direct his children and his house-
hold after him to keep the way of the LORD by doing what is
right and just, so that the LORD will bring about for Abra-
ham what he has promised him. (Genesis 18:17–19)

The commands of God were taught by Abraham to his household and the generations after him. If a man takes the responsibility to become the teacher and instructor in his home, he attracts God's favor and blessing. Why? Because the father functioning as teacher fulfills God's purpose for his life. Since the father is the source, everyone who comes out of him must look to him for instruction. God teaches the father to teach the future generations.

Look again at Adam and Eve in Genesis 1–3. Eve was taken out of Adam. She was designed and fashioned to be a receiver, but she received from the wrong source when she listened to Satan, who came to her in the form of a serpent in order to deceive her. The male is a giver, and the female is a receiver and an incubator. The woman does not initiate; she responds. She gives to her children as she has received from her husband, who is also her father. The man gives seed to the woman, and she gives back to the man a child. She takes what a man gives her, multiplies it, and gives it back. What incubators do is give life to the seed.

Herein lies a key principle: Whatever seed the father plants and whatever he teaches, that seed and instruction will be birthed through the mother to the children and the children's children. So, whatever Eve gave back to Adam was supposed to have been an increase and multiplication of that which Adam gave her in the first place. But Eve broke the principle. She went to Adam with something he never gave her. She had received from a source other than the right source.

God's purpose was distorted. God imparted to Adam, Adam instructed Eve, but Eve went to another source for teaching and instruction. Consequently, instead of bringing back fruit of life, Eve offered Adam the fruit of death. Then, when Adam accepted that fruit instead of reinforcing the instructions God had given him, humanity fell and sin entered the world.

Truth and life come from God the Father. Lies and destruction are what the devil gives. It is no wonder, then, that when Adam and Eve had children, one of the firstfruits of their offspring was hate and murder. Their son Cain killed their son Abel in a jealous rage. Adam and Eve had accepted information from a source not of God and they reproduced what they had received—death.

> **If the father has taught his wife and children the things of God, then godly lives will be produced in his children's children.**

Let's apply this principle to our families. Our children are supposed to bring back to us all that we have deposited into them. Often, the only way for a father to know how well he has done is by his grandchildren. If the father has taught his wife and children the things of God, then godly lives will be produced in his children's children. But if the father is absent or fails to teach the principles and precepts of the truth from the Word of God, then sin will likely be the fruit of his children's children. It's that simple. That is the awesome power of the father as a teacher.

> *Do not be deceived: God cannot be mocked. A man reaps what he sows. The one who sows to please his sinful nature, from that nature will reap destruction; the one who sows to*

please the Spirit, from the Spirit will reap eternal life.
(Galatians 6:7–8)

A wife and mother will bear good fruit when her husband sows into her the fruit of the Spirit. In contrast, we see the results of sowing into a woman the works of the flesh. Fathers who sow abuse will reap abuse. Fathers who sow addiction frequently have addicted wives and children. Fathers who sow divorce reap broken families. But fathers who sow the seed of the Spirit's fruit reap love, joy, peace, patience, kindness, goodness, faithfulness, gentleness, and self-control. (See Galatians 5:22–23.)

Fathers are to teach only the truth they hear from God the Father. As the perfect example of a teacher, Jesus asserted, "When you have lifted up the Son of Man, then you will know that I am the one I claim to be and that I do nothing on my own but speak just what the Father has taught me" (John 8:28). All that the Son taught came from His Father, the Source. What a powerful force a father is in his family when his wife and children know that whenever he acts or speaks, he is hearing from God.

The godly father doesn't react in anger toward his children by calling them names like *fool, idiot,* or *stupid.* Why not? Because the Father never calls him those names. The godly father speaks to his children only what he has heard from the Father. He calls his children saints, holy ones, priests, royalty, children of God, and sons of the Most High God. The father declares to his wife and children the image of God in Christ Jesus.

Remember the example of David and Solomon? Solomon did not teach his own wisdom but the wisdom he had learned from his father:

Listen, my sons, to a father's instruction; pay attention and gain understanding. I give you sound learning, so do not forsake my teaching. When I was a boy in my father's house, still tender, and an only child of my mother, he [David] *taught me* [Solomon] *and said, "Lay hold of my words with all your heart; keep my commands and you will live. Get wisdom, get understanding; do not forget my words or swerve from them."* (Proverbs 4:1–5)

David taught Solomon the wisdom and truth he learned from God. Solomon learned to value wisdom and passed it along to those who came after him. When he became king, he asked the heavenly Father to give him even greater wisdom to rule the nation. (See 2 Chronicles 1:9–12.)

The Father Instructs and the Mother Commands

Solomon said, *"My son, hear the instruction of thy father* [original information], *and forsake not the law of thy mother* [commands of the original information]*"* (Proverbs 1:8 KJV). There is a difference between an instruction and a command or law. Instruction is the giving or receiving of original information for direction and function. A command or law is a repetition and enforcement of instruction. In a godly context, an instruction is the truth that a father has learned from the Father. He imparts that instruction to his wife. As a mother, she repeats what she has heard as a command.

When I was growing up, there were eleven children in our family. One mother, one father, and eleven kids lived under one roof. My father worked all the time, but he was always at home in the voice of my mother. My mother never had to say, "If you don't do what I say, I will discipline you." All she had to say to keep the house in order was, "Do this and do that. If you don't, I will let your father know when he comes home." She always had the authority of his instructions. My father would say to the children, "You wash the dishes today. You clean the floor. You mow the lawn." We would pray together as a family, and then he would go to work.

That's it. He didn't have to be home to assert his authority because my mother was home. When she was in a meeting with some of her friends, all she had to do was look at me and say, "Myles, your father said to wash the dishes. Paul, you father said to clean the floor." She was simply giving commands. When she said, "Wash the dishes," I didn't hear her, I heard my father! I knew that if I disobeyed her commands, I also would be disobeying my father, even though he was not physically present at that moment. Dad gave the instruction, and Mom issued the law and gave the command. She repeated and enforced the instruction of my father. She invoked the authority of my father, and could say to me, "If you don't obey me, wait until your father comes home. He'll take care of you." That was enough! Believe me, I got the message. I had to comply, or else! I immediately did my chores. No questions were asked and no excuses were given, because I knew that behind my mother's command was my father's power and authority. He would bring judgment and discipline to my life if I failed to keep my mother's law. A woman is designed to rule by delegated authority.

> The father gets his original instruction and information from God the Father and His Word.

Once more, the father's instruction is original information. The mother's law or command is a repetition of the father's original teaching. This simple principle has been ignored in our society. We have homes where women are giving commands but have never received instructions. The children do not feel any authority or sense any power in mom's voice because there is no man in the house. As a result, there is lawlessness and rebellion in the home in the behavior and attitudes of the children. The father is really the key to healing the whole society and fixing the family. In his family, he must return to his God-given function of being a teacher like the Father who teaches him.

Where, then, does the father get his original instruction and information? From God the Father and His Word. Even if a father has not been fathered by a godly man, he can return to our heavenly Father, be saved, and learn God's ways. He can receive godly instruction from his pastor and righteous men in the church who know and love the Word of God. And, of course, as a born-again believer, a father has the Holy Spirit within him teaching him everything that the Son hears from the Father. (See John 16:5–15.)

A father who did not have a godly father from whom he was able to learn the Word of God should get under the spiritual authority of a pastor who teaches the Word. Daily, a father should submit in his relationship with God. He now has the heavenly Father—not an earthly father—to correct all the things he lacks in his own life. His family now has a teacher again.

The Teacher Spirit

Fathers are built to teach; again, that explains why males have difficulty being taught by women. Instructions are supposed to come from the father. God created the man to give instruction and the woman to receive his teaching and then command the children. Even when men have nothing to teach, they hate to admit that they don't have the answers.

One of the problems our society has is that it believes the cliche, "I learned all that I know at my mother's feet." We should not be receiving instructions from our mothers. Solomon's approach is God's way. The father instructs, and the mother commands what the father has taught.

Once again, go back to the original foundation established in Genesis. It would have made no sense for Eve to have taught Adam about the Tree of Knowledge of Good and Evil. She knew nothing about it. God the Father taught Adam, and Adam taught Eve.

Notice in Genesis 2:16–17 that *"the LORD God commanded the man, 'You are free to eat from any tree in the garden; but you must not eat from the tree of the knowledge of good and evil, for when you eat of it you will surely die.'"* God commanded the man—Adam—what to do. We can discern from Genesis 3:1–3 that Eve knew about that instruction. How? Adam taught her what God had said.

Adam did a good job teaching Eve, but, as we saw, she started getting instruction from someone who was not her father. There is another lesson about teaching here. Eve was supposed to accept, obey, and believe what Adam, her source, had said because Adam had received his information from the Father. However, she decided to forego what she had heard from her "father" and began to receive and listen to the teaching of one who was not her "father." The father should teach his wife and offspring not to receive instructions from any source other than the heavenly Father.

This is a very important principle: If children can learn to compare the information they receive in books, magazines, and the electronic media to God's truth, which they learned from their fathers, then they can go anywhere and face anything in culture and still know the truth.

Although I encountered a myriad of diverse and spurious philosophies in college, my father had already spoken the truth to me, rooted in the Father and His Word. That truth became the standard by which I measured everything. If Eve had compared what the serpent said to what Adam had already told her, she would have known immediately that the serpent was lying. Instead, she accepted the serpent's lie without checking it against the truth taught to her by Adam. She received instruction from a source other than the Father and, consequently, was deceived.

> **Children should be taught to compare the media content they receive with God's truth.**

The godly father should always emphasize to his wife and children that what he has learned is not only from his earthly father, but also from his heavenly Father. It's the standard. A father like the Father desires that this be said of him: *"As long as he lived, they* [his family and descendants] *did not fail to follow the LORD, the God of their fathers"* (2 Chronicles 34:33).

As a father teaching my children, I am not serving my father but the God of my fathers. I am serving the God of my spiritual fathers—Abraham, Isaac, Jacob, Joseph, Moses, David, and the prophets. I am serving the Father of my Lord Jesus Christ. So when my wife, children, and grandchildren follow my teaching, they are following the Word of God. My children know that the credibility of what I teach isn't just based on the fact that I said it, but that God said it!

What about Saved Wives and Their Unsaved Husbands?

I hear some women in churches say, "I'm going to do this or that because the pastor said to do this or that. I'm going to do this area of ministry. I'm going to serve in this way. Now, my husband doesn't agree with me or believe I should do this, but I'm following God and my church, not my husband." How should this attitude be addressed?

The moment a woman takes a husband, she has become his "offspring." Remember that Adam's offspring was Eve. Adam said, *"This* [the woman] *is now bone of my bones and flesh of my flesh; she shall be called 'woman,' for she was taken out of man"* (Genesis 2:23). Then the next statement reveals, *"For this reason a man will leave his father and mother and be united to his wife, and they will become one flesh"* (v. 24). It's important to note once more that nowhere in Scripture does it say a woman should leave her father. Only the man leaves his father and mother. Both Jesus and Paul quoted this verse in their teachings about marriage. The implication is that a woman, in effect, is never without a "father." Why? Because men are fathers. So when a woman is born into a home, she's under the authority of her father. When she gets married, she's under the authority of her other "father," her husband. She goes from one father to another because the male is her source and sustainer.

Again, Paul affirmed this principle when he wrote, *"For man did not come from woman, but woman from man; neither was man created for woman, but woman for man"* (1 Corinthians 11:8-9).

When Paul said, therefore, that a man does not cover his head, he was speaking about authority. (See 1 Corinthians 11:3-16.) Why? Because the man is the "father," and the woman should be under the covering of authority. To a woman, the man is both source and sustainer. Woman was created to receive, and man was created to give, instruct, and cover the woman.

Remember our question: What if a woman leaves her husband's authority to do what a church or pastor says? As a pastor, I cannot enter another man's house. He is his wife's husband, father, covering, and authority. I cannot instruct another woman to go against the authority of her husband. If I did, I would be acting as the serpent did in the garden with Eve. Much correction in the church is needed here. Pastors and church leaders should never usurp the authority of husbands and fathers.

Take a perfect example of this situation. In John 4, Jesus met the woman at the well. He is God, and He certainly could have worked a miracle right there, saving her and instantly healing every area of her life, but He didn't. Why? He understood the principles and functions of fatherhood. So Jesus asked the woman a very simple question, one we often miss. He said, in effect, "Where is your husband?" Jesus was referring to her covering, authority, and father. Not even Jesus moved in to replace her husband. Her answer is interesting: *"I have no husband"* (v. 17). Jesus' response to this statement implied, "You are right. I know the ones you had, and the one you have now is not your husband. You are without a covering. I can help you. I can give you instructions." (See 1 Corinthians 11:17–18, 21–24.)

What does a pastor or church do when a wife is under the authority of an ungodly man? The church has made many mistakes in this area. Our ultimate goal in the church is not just to get a Christian woman into ministry. The goal of the church, according to Jesus, is to be fishers of men by going into all the world with the gospel. God is more concerned about that woman's unsaved husband being restored to Him than about that woman having a ministry in the church. The Great Commission given in Matthew 28:18–20 is not for the purpose of placing people in positions. It is for making disciples of all nations and saving the lost. Now, if that concept is clear, then we must do everything in our legal authority in the body of Christ to get that man saved. We should be encouraging and equipping the wife to witness to and love her husband as Christ loves her.

> As the bride of Christ, the church has the Father's instruction, authority, and power to speak and act with boldness.

It contradicts the Great Commission for the church to compete with the woman's husband, whom they should want to win to Christ. When a woman comes to me as a pastor and says, "Pastor, my husband says I cannot come to the meeting that you called, but you are my pastor. What should I do?" my answer is, "You stay with your husband because I am not your father." And I even go so far as to write a note to her husband, apologizing for my program conflicting with his schedule, and requesting that he please forgive me. I send his wife back to him.

How might that husband respond? He may well be led to Christ because now he says, "I've finally met a pastor who isn't trying to compete with me." He will desire to know more about the God that his wife serves. Why? Because neither God nor the church tries to take his wife from him, but rather teaches her to respect him as her husband and the father of their household. This is not to say that a woman should give up going to church altogether if her husband doesn't like it. She needs to have fellowship with other Christians. (See Hebrews 10:25.) Yet some women spend so much time at church that they neglect their husbands, and they don't show them love and respect.

Instruction Brings Power and Authority

Since a woman was not designed to give instructions, but to give commands, this means the woman's power is wrapped up in the man. As I mentioned earlier, the reason why the single mothers of our nations are having such a hard time is that they are giving commands but never receiving instructions. This is a key principle that has a broader application to Christ and His bride, the church.

As we have seen, one of the titles of Jesus is *"Everlasting Father"* (Isaiah 9:6). Another title used by those around Him was Rabbi or Teacher. What qualified Him to teach? He is a father who receives His instructions from God, His Father.

Jesus, the Second Adam, succeeded where the first Adam failed. Jesus listened to the Father and spoke only what the Father said. He also taught exactly what the Father wanted taught. Then, out of Jesus came a "woman"—the church, the *"ecclesia."* The bride of Christ, His church, does only what He says because the bride has the Holy Spirit, who speaks only what the Son has heard from the Father. (See John 14–16.) Notice the progression of teaching that Jesus delineated:

When the Counselor [Holy Spirit] *comes, whom I will send to you from the Father, the Spirit of truth who goes out from the Father, he will testify about me. And you also must testify, for you have been with me from the beginning.*

(John 15:26–27)

From the Father through the Son by the Spirit, we are taught the truth—which we, in turn, teach others. The only instructions we are supposed to speak are those from the Father, which we learn through reading His Word and listening to His Spirit. The church takes these instructions and speaks them out with authority as commands. This is the principle behind Jesus' statement regarding authority and how we can use His name to command sickness, disease, demons, and mountains.

> **Fathers have abandoned their responsibility to be teachers of the Word of God in their homes.**

As the bride of Christ, the church has the Father's instruction, authority, and power to speak and act with boldness in the world. The bride of Christ is empowered to declare things. "I bind you" is a command, not an instruction. "I loose you" is a command. "Come out of him" is a command. The church binds, looses, heals, and delivers, not as teachings, but as commands under the authority of our Husband, Jesus Christ, who taught us what He heard from the Father.

Christ gave us instructions, and then He left. We remain in the world with His instructions. We are supposed to go out and possess the land and take back what the devil has stolen. We have the authority of the Father to do so. When we command, lives change because the authority of the Father is in us through His Holy Spirit. We declare truth in His name because we have His authority.

Lack of Authority Leads to Confusion and Chaos

It is tragic that in many homes today, the mother cannot invoke the name of her child's father with authority. In fact, many curse the father's name. Why? Because fathers have abandoned their responsibility to be teachers of the Word of God in their homes.

We have seen that one of Satan's primary strategies is to remove fathers from the home. Satan attacks fathers because when they do what they were created to do, they teach about the Father in their homes. Satan hates that! He wants the home to be in rebellion against fathers and God the Father. If Satan can remove the teacher, there is no instruction. If there is no instruction, there is no authority. If there is no authority, there is anarchy and chaos. When there is anarchy and chaos, any number of undesirable things can happen—kids join gangs, get involved in drugs, and run with bad company—all because there is no authority in the home.

Since the father gives instruction in the home, he also must discipline and give correction to his household. We now turn to the father's function as the one who disciplines in the home.

CHAPTER PRINCIPLES

1. God teaches fathers, then fathers teach their households.

2. Whatever seed the father plants and whatever he teaches, that seed and instruction is birthed through the mother to the children and the children's children.

3. Earthly fathers are to teach only the truth they hear from the heavenly Father!

4. Fathers instruct and mothers command. The father's instruction is original information. The mother's law, or command, is a repetition of the father's original teaching.

5. The father should teach his wife and offspring not to receive spiritual truth from any source other than from the heavenly Father, through His Word and His Spirit.

6. Pastors and church leaders should not seek to usurp the authority of husbands. (This does not mean a woman should never attend church if her husband dislikes it, but she should demonstrate love and respect for him and not use church as an excuse to neglect him.)

7. As the bride of Christ, the church has the Father's instruction, authority, and power to speak and act with boldness in the world; the church commands what Jesus heard from the Father.

Chapter 7

FATHER AS ONE WHO DISCIPLINES

To understand what it means for the father to be one who disciplines, we must first realize that discipline is not punishment. Discipline takes teaching to the next level. It is one thing to teach a child, but correction and further instruction help to shape a child's character. Discipline, therefore, is training.

"Train a child in the way he should go, and when he is old he will not turn from it" (Proverbs 22:6). This instruction is spoken to fathers. Notice the application of this principle in Ephesians 6:4: *"Fathers, do not exasperate your children; instead, bring them up in the training and instruction of the Lord."* Again, I want to emphasize that discipline is not punishment rendered by an irate or enraged father. Paul clearly warned, *"Fathers, do not embitter your children, or they will become discouraged"* (Colossians 3:21).

What society has done is leave discipline to the women because most men think that training is punishment. In referring to woman, God said, *"It is not good that the man should be alone; I will make him an help meet for him"* (Genesis 2:18 KJV). To be a *"help meet"* means to be "suitable" or "adaptable." One who is suitable or adaptable can be trained and equipped in responsibility.

We read in Genesis 2:15, *"The LORD God took the man, and put him into the garden of Eden to dress ["cultivate" NASB] it and to keep it"* (KJV). This instruction refers to discipline and order. To *"dress"* means to *"cultivate,"* and to cultivate means to train.

A father is given the responsibility by God the Father to train and equip everything under his care, including his wife and children.

> When there is planning and training, we see discipline and cultivation taking place.

What is the difference between cultivation and mere growth? When plants grow without cultivation, they are essentially weeds. Cultivated plants form a garden. Trees that grow without cultivation and order are a forest. Cultivated trees are a grove. Without cultivation, there is no order and no systematic development. But when there is planning and training, we see discipline and cultivation taking place.

Genesis 2:5 reveals that cultivation is part of God the Father's plan for humanity. *"And no shrub of the field had yet appeared on the earth and no plant of the field had yet sprung up, for the LORD God had not sent rain on the earth and there was no man to work ["cultivate" NASB] the ground."* Adam's job description included cultivating the ground given to him for sustenance. God placed man in the garden and gave him instructions to work, train, and keep the earth; He did not want wild, unrestrained, and disorganized growth. God the

Father has an orderly, disciplined, and purposeful plan for everything.

As Adam was to cultivate the earth, a father is to cultivate his offspring. When Eve came along and eventually the children, Adam, as a father, was to make certain they did not grow wild. The world believes children need to "sow wild oats" as they grow up, but that is in direct contradiction to God's plan of cultivation and discipline. Today, we have boys throwing their seed—their sperm—all over the place because we are not cultivating and disciplining them. Our heavenly Father trains and disciplines us; likewise, fathers are to follow His example in the lives of their children.

The book of Hebrews says it in this way:

You have forgotten that word of encouragement that addresses you as sons: "My son, do not make light of the Lord's discipline, and do not lose heart when he rebukes you, because the Lord disciplines those he loves, and he punishes everyone he accepts as a son." Endure hardship as discipline; God is treating you as sons. For what son is not disciplined by his father? If you are not disciplined (and everyone undergoes discipline), then you are illegitimate children and not true sons. Moreover, we have all had human fathers who disciplined us and we respected them for it. How much more should we submit to the Father of our spirits and live! Our fathers disciplined us for a little while as they thought best; but God disciplines us for our good, that we may share in his holiness.

(Hebrews 12:5–10)

God the Father disciplines us, and fathers, like God, are to discipline their children.

Let me give you some examples of the ways in which fathers can discipline, cultivate, and train their children. Remember that the word *discipline* comes from the word *disciple*, which refers to one who learns by following. So fathers train and disciple their children by having them follow their example. Their children learn by imitation. That is exactly what Jesus had His disciples do. He told them, "Follow Me!" (See, for example, Matthew 4:19.)

> **Fathers train and disciple their children by having them follow their example.**

A concrete example of this concept is a train. We call an entire line of railroad cars on a track a "train." Yet *train* comes from a word meaning "to draw" or "to drag." Technically, only the engine is the train, because everything else attached to the engine is a follower. The principle that governs a train is similar to the principle God wants implemented in our families. A father is never supposed to just point his wife or children in a direction. He is the engine and should be able to say, "Hook up to me. Go where I am going. Follow me. Imitate my example, and then you'll be going in the right direction."

A father's primary responsibility is to be like the heavenly Father and to do what He does. God does not point one way but then go another. A true father never says, "Do what I say but not what I do." Instead, a godly father with integrity can unashamedly say to his wife and children, "Live the way I live, and you will be like the Father." In other words, a father becomes in Christ what he wants his wife and children to become.

Consider again the example of Abraham. Abraham received favor from God because he cultivated his household in God's commandments. (See Genesis 18:18–19.) He even cultivated his servant. He did not allow anyone to work in his household without being trained and disciplined in the ways of God. He made certain that even his servants obeyed God's standards and followed his example.

The principle is this: A father follows the example of the Father and teaches his offspring to follow him. A godly father leads everyone following him to the Father.

Abraham did not want a pagan working for him. Everyone in his household followed father Abraham, and Abraham followed God the Father.

Fathers must *disciple* their families. Again, a disciple is a follower who learns by observation. Disciples in the past always left home because learning was *living* life, not just talking about it. The father not only teaches in the home, but he also takes his children out into the world with him in order to have them observe how he handles various situations in a godly way. If a father is going to disciple his children, he must do so by letting them see how he functions in different conditions.

It is impossible to be effective as a long-distance father. A father cannot father children he is not with, or train children who are not by his side. You cannot disciple on the telephone or via e-mail. Not being present in his children's lives makes a man a biological supplier of sperm, not a father. A father trains a child by having the child observe what the father does, says, and decides in the real world.

Fathers need to discipline and disciple their households by letting their families observe them in the following ways:

- Reading and applying the Word of God.
- Praying and interceding.
- Making right decisions based on the principles and absolute truths of God's Word.
- Working in the real world, living out the example of Christ.
- Sharing the gospel with others.
- Openly worshiping and praising God the Father.
- Handling and solving problems without compromise.
- Being promise keepers and not promise breakers.
- Treating their wives with honor and dignity.
- Honoring others above themselves.
- Loving their enemies.
- Being reconcilers between races and economic classes.
- Making sure that their words and actions correspond—and exhibit character and integrity.

In ancient Israel, the disciples followed their rabbis everywhere, learning to live by their examples. In a similar way, when fathers disciple their children, they show them how to live life by their example. The father becomes a master in his own household; that is not a negative description. As the father masters the skills and gifts of operating in the power of the Holy Spirit, the family members can observe the master and learn for themselves how to walk in the Spirit.

Our next step toward understanding the functions of fatherhood is to examine how the father is the head and leader of his home.

CHAPTER PRINCIPLES

1. Fathers are given by God the responsibility to train and equip everything under their care.

2. God the Father disciplines us, and godly fathers discipline their children.

3. When fathers train their children, they teach by example, thereby enabling their children to learn by imitation.

4. A father follows the example of our heavenly Father and teaches his offspring to follow him. A godly father thus leads everyone following him to God.

5. Men cannot be fathers to children they are not with, or train children who are not by their side. A father trains a child by having the child observe what the father does, says, and decides in the real world.

6. Fathers need to disciple their households by allowing their families to observe them operating in a godly manner and in the power of the Holy Spirit.

Chapter 8

FATHER AS HEAD AND LEADER

One of the Latin words for father is *fundus*, which means "base" or "bottom." This is where we get the word *foundation*. We talked about the male as foundation in chapter two. The foundation of the family is the father who begins as the progenitor and source and then sustains, nourishes, protects, teaches, and disciplines his household.

The father is the head of the family as a result of God's timing and creation. Now, the fact that he is the head does not mean he is superior, better, or greater than the woman. It means that he has first responsibility and accountability for the family.

Again, being the head is not a value statement about worth or intrinsic value. The father can never say that being the head or leader makes him the greatest. Jesus as Head of the church humbled Himself as a servant: *"Your attitude should be the same as that of Christ Jesus: who, being in very nature God, did not consider equality with God something to be grasped, but made himself nothing, taking the very nature of a servant, being made in human likeness"* (Philippians 2:5–7).

Heads and leaders are first and foremost servants like Christ. It is impossible to assume a position of leadership without first serving. Jesus said,

> *You know that those who are regarded as rulers of the Gentiles lord it over them, and their high officials exercise authority over them. Not so with you. Instead, whoever wants to become great among you must be your servant, and whoever wants to be first must be slave of all. For even the Son of Man did not come to be served, but to serve, and to give his life as a ransom for many.*   (Mark 10:42–45)

We can use the physical body as an analogy for understanding the spiritual functions of being the head of the family. The head plans for the care of the body and, in general, guides the body's actions. Many men love to say, "I'm the head of this house," but they forget the accountability and duty of being the head. The father has the responsibility to preserve, protect, nourish, and guide his wife and children.

Fathers Plan

First, the "head" contains the brain. If the man claims to be the father and head of the home, then he must have the mind of Christ (see 1 Corinthians 2:16), which includes the knowledge and wisdom to lead a family in the ways of God. The father has the responsibility to solve the problems the family encounters. He calculates where the family is going and seeks God's guidance to make long-term plans—ten, fifteen, or twenty years—for the family. The father is the counselor, career and financial planner, and manager of the family's resources. All those functions are in the brain. Fingers and legs do not make those kinds of decisions; they are made in the brain.

Fathers Provide Vision

The father, if he is truly the head, becomes the visionary of the family. The eyes are in the head and they see what's in front of the body. The eyes are not in the back or in the stomach. If you are the head, you are supposed to have a vision for your family: insight, long-range goals, and a plan for the future. The father discerns things that are happening in the natural as well as the supernatural for the family.

As the visionary, the father anticipates things before they happen and prepares and equips the family to face the future. Fathers have *perception, conception,* and *inception.*

Perception:

Perception is awareness of what's going on. A father knows what's happening with his wife and children at all times. When behaviors or attitudes change, he knows it. When spiritual or physical needs

> As the visionary, the father prepares and equips the family to face the future.

arise, he is aware of them. Nothing escapes his attention. The father is tuned-in and cares about each person in his family. Too often I hear families complain, "Dad just isn't with it. He never knows or understands what's happening in our lives. He's too wrapped up in his work to notice us." Remember, God cares about everything. Jesus was aware of everything that happened around Him, even to the point of noticing a woman in need barely touching the hem of His garment. (See Mark 5:24–34.) God the Father is aware of all things. Jeremiah prayed, *"Great are your purposes and mighty are your deeds. Your eyes are open to all the ways of men; you reward everyone according to his conduct and as his deeds deserve"* (Jeremiah 32:19). Like the Father, a father is aware of all that happens in his family.

Conception:

Conception is the creative beginning of a process, which puts in motion a chain of events. God sets everything in motion; He is *"the God who made the world and everything in it"* (Acts 17:24). He initiates, conceives, and creates. Likewise, a father conceives in his mind the beginnings of things for his family and then becomes the source for bringing what he has conceived into reality. As the head of the family, he takes the initiative to listen to God and conceive *God's* ideas, not just what seem like good ideas.

Inception:

Inception is the start or commencement of something new. God the Father is always doing "a new thing" in our lives. He said, *"See, I am doing a new thing! Now it springs up; do you not perceive it? I am making a way in the desert and streams in the wasteland"* (Isaiah 43:19). A father is willing to risk new things for his family. He will break out of old traditions and bondages. A father receives the words God has for him and his family, rejoicing in the refreshing newness of God's river in his life.

Fathers Discern

What else is in the head? The nose. The nose discerns and detects. Are you a father who is always discerning? Discerning is related to caring, which we will discuss in the next chapter. A godly father can sense what is coming against his family in the next several years. He also has a sense of what is going to happen next week; he detects and addresses what is going on with his children. Perhaps his teenager is experiencing some tough changes and tremendous peer pressure. As the head of the household, he discerns the problem and spends time with that child to counsel, support, affirm, and advise. A godly father also senses when his wife is in need of affection or time alone. In other words, a father can detect the "scent" of his family, his home, his business, and his neighborhood.

God the Father knew our needs and prepared for us before the foundation of the world:

Praise be to the God and Father of our Lord Jesus Christ, who has blessed us in the heavenly realms with every spiritual blessing in Christ. For he chose us in him before the creation of the world to be holy and blameless in his sight. In love he predestined us to be adopted as his sons through Jesus Christ, in accordance with his pleasure and will—to the praise of his glorious grace, which he has freely given us in the One he loves. In him we have redemption through his blood, the forgiveness of sins, in accordance with the riches of God's grace that he lavished on us with all wisdom and understanding. And he made known to us the mystery of his will according to his good pleasure, which he purposed in Christ, to be put into effect when the times will have reached their fulfillment—to bring all things in heaven and on earth together under one head, even Christ. In him we were also chosen, having been predestined according to the plan of him who works out everything in conformity with the purpose of his will, in order that we, who were the first to hope in Christ, might be for the praise of his glory. And you also were included in Christ when you heard the word of truth, the gospel of your salvation. Having believed, you were marked in him with a seal, the promised Holy Spirit, who is a deposit guaranteeing our inheritance until the redemption of those who are God's possession—to the praise of his glory. (Ephesians 1:3-14)

God prepared (1) for Christ to die for our sins, (2) for the gift of the Holy Spirit, and (3) for our eternal inheritance in glory. Now that's a real father! God discerned our need before we were ever created. Jesus was sensing our need before His crucifixion and resurrection. He said, *"In my Father's house are many rooms; if it were not so, I would have told you. I am going there to prepare a place for you"* (John 14:2).

Consider Adam in the garden before Eve was created from him. God anticipated man's loneliness. Adam didn't know he was alone. He had the garden, all the creatures of the earth, and most of all, he had God. Adam could not possibly have been lonely because he dwelled within God's presence; however, God knew the purpose and nature of the man He had created. God the Father anticipated Adam's need before he even had it; therefore, God created Eve.

Fathers Listen

Also located on the head are the ears. You are a father if you can hear for your family. The father should always be listening to God and to his family, for God the Father always listens to us. The psalmist wrote, *"I love the LORD, for he heard my voice; he heard my cry for mercy. Because he turned his ear to me, I will call on him as long as I live"* (Psalm 116:1). I hear wives and children continually complain, "Dad never has time to listen to me." Fathers, please take time to listen. As a father and head of the family, here are some questions you need to answer for yourself:

- Are you hearing the voice of God?
- Are you getting instructions for yourself and for the family's sake?
- Are you getting information for your wife and the children?
- Are you picking up on what's going on in the world and preparing your family to face it?
- Are you hearing correction, instruction, and rebuke?
- Are you hearing the true voice of your wife and children?

Many men think they are too busy to listen to their families. Yet listening is a gift that fathers give to their families. Their listening tells their families that they care for them, while a failure to listen communicates a lack of love and caring. Because God the Father loves us, He always listens to and answers us. We fathers need to listen as our heavenly Father listens!

Fathers Speak the Word of God

Finally, being the head means that the father is the mouthpiece for the family. The father is supposed to speak the Word of God in the home. Through the father's voice, the family hears God's voice.

If a wife wants to hear from God, she should be able to hear His voice through a godly husband first, and not only the pastor, prophet, apostle, teacher, or evangelist in the church.

Likewise, if the children want to hear what God is saying, they shouldn't go to somebody else first. The family should hear from God through the head of the family, who is himself able to hear from God and who knows His Word. Everything said at church should confirm and support what has already been said at home by the father who is in close relationship with the heavenly Father.

For example, Paul said that women should be silent in the church.

> *Women should remain silent in the churches. They are not allowed to speak, but must be in submission, as the Law says. If they want to inquire about something, they should ask their own husbands at home; for it is disgraceful for a woman to speak in the church.*
>
> (1 Corinthians 14:34–35)

It is important to understand the full context of this Scripture in order to appreciate the true value and impact of Paul's admonition.

In the church meetings at Corinth, there were many problems. This was because some of the people who converted to the Christian faith came from prostitution and pagan practices. Some of the services were at risk of becoming wild or uncontrollable if those new converts reverted to their old pagan practices. Furthermore, in the synagogues, men and women were separated. The men would sit in the main area while the women would sit behind them or in a balcony. In this setting, many women would call out to their husbands questions about what the rabbi was teaching.

First, Paul was saying that God wants order and decency in the church. Second, it was not culturally appropriate for a woman to speak in public. And third, Paul knew that when the wife went home, she could then ask her husband to answer her questions about what had been taught. The implication is that the husband should know the answer. In fact, the husband should have anticipated his wife's questions and taught her the Word or law before she went to the synagogue.

Yes, a woman has ministry gifts and should exercise them. The problem with women speaking in the church was a male problem. When fathers and husbands fulfilled their responsibilities as the head of the home, women did not have to ask questions in the middle of a service. They received their answers from the head of the family, who spoke with God's voice to the family.

The Father as Leader

As I said earlier, being the head of the family does not impart more worth or value to the man. Being the head has to do with responsibility. Too many men confuse being the head with being the boss. A father is not the boss of his house; a father is the head. A father doesn't rule his house; he leads his house. We must understand the function of the father as leader in the home.

Let me share with you some qualities of leadership the father has in the home:

- As leader, the father has a passion and desire to bring out the best in all those under his care: his wife, children, and any other family members.

- A true leader does not suppress, oppress, or depress the potential and talents of others; he releases them and cultivates them.

- A true leader provides an environment for growth. He does not try to inhibit family members or create an atmosphere of fear. A true leader's passion is to maximize the potential of others so they may realize their full and true abilities; his goal is to eventually work himself out of a job.

In a very true sense, a father who is a genuine leader does exactly what God said to do from the beginning—he cultivates. To cultivate means to create an orderly environment that brings out the best in a thing, to culture it. As a leader, the father develops, expands, instigates, motivates, inspires, encourages, and exhorts. All those functions cultivate the soil in which others grow.

"I am the true vine, and my Father is the gardener. He cuts off every branch in me that bears no fruit, while every branch that does bear fruit he prunes so that it will be even more fruitful" (John 15:1-2). Jesus taught that the Gardener (the Father) cultivates the Vine's (the Son's) branches (believers, or the church) so they can bear spiritual fruit. Likewise, the earthly father is to cultivate his family.

Jesus is the Head of the church, His bride. He loves and gives Himself for her continuously. In the same way, a father, as head of his family, loves and gives himself daily for his wife and children.

> *Speaking the truth in love, we will in all things grow up into him who is the Head, that is, Christ.* (Ephesians 4:15)

> *For the husband is the head of the wife as Christ is the head of the church, his body, of which he is the Savior.* (Ephesians 5:23)

Now let us turn our attention to the caring function of the father for his family. As head and leader of the family, the father also deeply cares for his family in every area of their lives.

CHAPTER PRINCIPLES

1. Heads and leaders are first and foremost servants like Christ. It is impossible to assume a position of leadership without first serving.

2. Fathers must have the mind of Christ (see 1 Corinthians 2:16), which includes the knowledge and wisdom to lead a family in the ways of God.

3. As the visionary, the father anticipates things before they happen and prepares and equips the family to face the future. Fathers have perception, conception, and inception.

4. Fathers discern and address the ongoing needs of their families.

5. Listening is a gift that fathers give to their families. When men listen, their listening tells their families that they care for them.

6. A true father speaks the Word of God in the home. Through the father's voice, the family is able to hear God's voice.

7. A father doesn't dominate or control his house. He develops the potential of everyone in his house through his leadership.

Chapter 9

FATHER AS ONE
WHO CARES

I n many ways, the father's functions of caring and developing go hand in hand. His role as one who cares is rooted in Genesis 2:15: *"And the LORD God took the man, and put him in the garden of Eden to dress* ["cultivate" NASB] *it and to keep it"* (KJV). Once more, the word *"dress"* in this verse means to *"cultivate."* The word *"keep"* means to care for. To care is to pay close attention to needs and also to meet those needs. In fact, caring goes far beyond our normal thoughts of serving, encouraging, and ministering to someone.

Anticipating Needs and Meeting Them

Again, the word *care* means to anticipate a need and meet it. In other words, to care means that you calculate the next need of a person before he or she is aware of it. You make provisions before he or she even senses the need. I believe that is the kind of caring that Psalm 8:4 describes: *"What is man that you are mindful of him, the son of man that you care for him?"* To be mindful means to have one's mind filled with thoughts about another person. God the Father has filled His thoughts with us. He anticipates and thinks about what we will need before we even need it.

Jesus taught us that our Father cares deeply for us:

So do not worry, saying, "What shall we eat?" or "What shall we drink?" or "What shall we wear?" For the pagans run after all these things, and your heavenly Father knows that you need them. But seek first his kingdom and his righteousness, and all these things will be given to you as well.
(Matthew 6:31–33)

The Father knows our needs and cares about us.

A father, like God the Father, cares by spending his time and energy anticipating what his wife and children need next. This is the most beautiful picture in the world of a father. No matter what he is doing, he is constantly thinking about what his daughter will need the next day, what his son will need the next week, or what his wife will need the next year. He's constantly thinking about caring for his family.

> **A father who cares like the Father thinks of his wife and children before his job.**

Work-driven cultures try to force men to continually think about what the company or corporation needs, so that they have no time to think about anyone else's needs. Men no longer work to live, but live to work. Even at home, a man's mind is often drifting off to work and either solving problems or thinking of new projects. Or, the father comes home so tired from working that he dozes off in front of the television. Meanwhile, his family is left neglected and uncared for because he is too tired or busy to think about their needs.

Fathers must set the right priorities. A father who cares like the Father thinks of his wife and children before his job.

A father should see his job as a gift from God that enables him to care for his wife and children. In other words, God's care has provided the man with a job so that he can adequately care for the physical needs of his family. The job is a means to an end, never the end itself.

Men who are wrapped up in their careers and running after the corporate world have their motivation and priorities out of place. They have taken their work, a gift from God that He intended to help support their families, and made it an idol. They end up caring more about the gift than the family for which it was given or the God who gave it. Such idolatry will ruin the man and his family.

Pastors as Fathers

One model that our churches often look to for fathering is the pastor. I want to address a concern I have about pastors modeling fatherhood for their people. In our society, pastors have a growing divorce rate. Many could be properly classified as "workaholics." Often, pastors' wives feel helpless in trying to turn their husbands' hearts back toward home. The pastor seems to care for everyone else before his family. To defend his workaholism, a pastor may say to his wife, "You know I'm doing this for the church. This is my calling. I'm doing this for the Lord." Unable to compete with God, the family members desperately try to get their needs met inappropriately and may even end up blaming God for their father caring more for the church than for his family. The church then becomes a "mistress" to the pastor, as he leaves wife and family to suffer without him.

Laypeople also need to take this caution to heart, for they are often a major cause of the pastor's problems. They expect the pastor to be Christ and not simply the pastor. The man of God can never take the place of Christ caring for His bride. Too often, church members turn to the pastor to meet their needs instead of to the Lord. As a result, the demands on the pastor's counseling, calling, and visitation become unrealistic. Only Christ is omnipresent, omniscient, and ommnipotent—not the pastor.

The answer to this dilemma is simple and clear. It's found in Ephesians 5, where the principles are laid down by Paul concerning Christ and His bride, and the husband and his wife. Here's a statement from Paul that wraps it up: *"Husbands, love your wives, just as Christ loved the church and gave himself up for her"* (Ephesians 5:25). Pastors, and not just laymen, are to love their wives as Christ loved the church.

> **When church members expect the pastor to take the place of Christ, the demands on his time become unrealistic.**

As I said before, some pastors are committing "adultery" with their churches. As a pastor, I am not married to my church; I'm married to my wife. The "woman" that I oversee—the assembly of believers—is not my wife—she's Christ's wife. Ultimately, who meets the church's emotional needs? Not me. Who meets her physical needs? Not me. Who meets her temporal needs? Not me. Who meets her spiritual needs? Not me. Christ meets all the needs of His wife, the church. Some pastors are destroying their wives and children because they are spending all their time and energy trying to do what only Christ can do.

As far as the church is concerned, pastors should be the prime examples of fathers caring for their families. Again, one of the reasons we have so many broken homes among pastors is that they cared more for their work than their families. We see pastors' children who are wayward, disoriented, confused, and backslidden because the pastor was not a father. He did not care for his family. Husbands, love your wives as Christ loves the church, and care for your children as the heavenly Father cares for you.

> **Within the church, pastors should be prime examples of fathers caring for their children.**

A father's care, therefore, is one of his major functions. He sits down and calculates the upcoming needs of his family and then plans and works to meet those needs. He does not allow his job to overwhelm his relationship with his family. He pays attention to the interests, desires, and fears of his wife and children and shows concern for them.

In the next chapter, we will explore the final function of fathering: the male as developer of his family.

CHAPTER PRINCIPLES

1. A father, like God the Father, cares by spending his time and energy anticipating what his wife and children will need next.

2. A man's job is a gift from God that He intended to help care for that man's family. When a father places more importance on his work than his family, he makes an idol out of his work and will bring ruin upon himself and his family.

3. Fathers must set the right priorities. A father who cares like the Father thinks of his wife and children before his job.

4. Pastors should be the prime examples of fathers caring for their families.

5. Both pastors and laymen are to love their wives as Christ loved the church.

Chapter 10

FATHER AS DEVELOPER

The father is called to develop his family. To develop means "to cause to grow gradually and continually in fuller, larger, and better ways." God the Father develops His people. Consider what Paul said about the Father:

> *I planted the seed, Apollos watered it, but God made it grow. So neither he who plants nor he who waters is anything, but only God, who makes things grow. The man who plants and the man who waters have one purpose, and each will be rewarded according to his own labor. For we are God's fellow workers; you are God's field.*
>
> (1 Corinthians 3:6–9)

To understand the father as developer, we return again to the garden of Eden and remember God's instructions to Adam to *"dress"* and *"keep"* it (Genesis 2:15 KJV). In dressing and keeping the garden, Adam had to plan for the orderly growth of both plant and animal life. Developing for order and cultivation started when Adam named the animals. (See verses 19–20.)

The Characteristics of Development

Development has these characteristics:

Planning

Inherent in God's purpose is His plan. Before a developer starts constructing a housing division or shopping complex, he has a building plan. He presents the plan to the appropriate governmental officials in order to obtain the required permits to build. The plan includes what will be constructed as well as how it will be used. Structure and usage are essential to a plan. For example, the Father as Developer planned the garden and also planned what would be in it. God structured streams to come up from the earth in order to water the garden. He provided food for Adam and Eve, had a plan concerning what they could and could not eat, and gave specific usage instructions to Adam.

> *Then God said, I give you every seed-bearing plant on the face of the whole earth and every tree that has fruit with seed in it. They will be yours for food....And the LORD God commanded the man, "You are free to eat from any tree in the garden; but you must not eat from the tree of the knowledge of good and evil, for when you eat of it you will surely die."* (Genesis 1:29; 2:16–17)

Preparing and Planting

Once there is a plan, the developer begins the necessary groundwork for building. Earthmovers come in and drainage is provided. The land is prepared to accept the building—first a foundation and then a framework. Likewise, a sower prepares the soil and sows the seed in planning for a harvest.

*"Now the L*ord *God had planted a garden in the east, in Eden; and there he put the man he had formed"* (Genesis 2:8).

Protecting

Every developer protects his construction site. He may construct a tall fence with barbed wire to keep out intruders. He may hire security guards. The farmer who develops a crop uses whatever means of protection his crop needs to guard against insects, diseases, and vandals. He tends the crop by pulling weeds and providing adequate irrigation. God the Developer protected man by warning him not to eat from the Tree of Knowledge of Good and Evil and giving him instructions on what to do in the garden. God also walked with Adam and Eve in the cool of the evening. (See Genesis 3:8.) Keeping in fellowship with God was protection for them.

Producing

Once a building is finished, the developer uses his shopping complex, houses, or commercial building to produce income. The farmer who grows a crop doesn't just leave it in the field. He harvests it because he has produced fruits or vegetables that can be sold and used. Likewise, the Father develops us to be productive in His plan and purpose. Jesus addressed this issue of development very specifically: *"This is to my Father's glory, that you bear much fruit, showing yourselves to be my disciples"* (John 15:8).

Like the Father, an earthly father develops his wife and children. He plans their growth in every aspect of life—physically, intellectually, emotionally, and spiritually.

A father walks each step of the way with his family as he prepares and equips them in the ways of God. He plants the seed of God's Word in their hearts. He protects them with prayer and with his presence and provision for their lives. As a godly father walks with his family, he is an example of holiness for them. He expects the best from them in producing good fruit, which gives glory to the Father. He develops his offspring to glow with the glory of God. A father expects his family to be the light of the world, the salt of the earth, and witnesses for Christ in the world.

> A father encourages steady, consistent, progressive growth in his family.

Light produces light. The light of Christ in a father's life sets his family ablaze for Christ. The prayer of every godly father is that his children will become flames of fire, blazing with the Father's Spirit and shining as stars. *"Those who are wise will shine like the brightness of the heavens, and those who lead many to righteousness, like the stars for ever and ever"* (Daniel 12:3).

The Environment for Development

As a father develops his offspring, he disciples them by providing an example of the Father. He encourages steady, consistent, and progressive growth in his family. For example, he will not give answers all the time but will show his children where to find the answers. A father like the Father encourages discovery and learning as part of the developmental process.

Development creates an environment that is conducive to others encountering learning experiences under the guidance of a father's godly wisdom. So what does an environment that encourages development and growth look like? Let me share with you some environmental qualities of a father who develops his offspring:

Encouragement

The father edifies his offspring. *"Therefore encourage one another and build each other up, just as in fact you are doing"* (1 Thessalonians 5:11). Fathers never tear down the esteem of a family member. Paul wrote that God gave him power to edify, not to destroy. (See 2 Corinthians 13:10.) Such is the power that God gives fathers—to build up their families, not pull them down.

Positive feedback

Instead of criticism, a father like the Father gives constructive correction. He develops his wife and children by building on their strengths and focusing on what they can do well instead of condemning them for their weaknesses. In fact, the father bears the weaknesses of his family. (See Romans 15:1 KJV.) He covers—not exposes—their vulnerability, and he protects them from attack with his own prayers and instructions.

Opportunity to try and fail

Fathers understand that some of the most significant learning experiences in life result from failure. Children can learn from their failures if a father uses the failures for teaching and correction instead of judgment and punishment. A father develops an atmosphere of acceptance for his family. He will not reject them just because they tried and failed. He accepts his family "for better or worse," just as Christ has accepted him. *"Accept one another, then, just as Christ accepted you, in order to bring praise to God"* (Romans 15:7).

Does not make comparisons

A father understands that the only standard for life is Jesus Christ. He never compares his wife or children to others, thinking that, by making a comparison, he will force improvement. A father never says to his son or daughter, "Why can't you be more like So-and-so? They are such good kids and never cause their parents any trouble. They make such good grades in school; why can't you?" He never says to his wife, "Why can't you dress and look like So-and-so? She is such a good cook and helpmate. Why can't you be more like her?" Such comments by a father come from the father of lies. Satan desires that we compare ourselves and our families to others so that he can divide families and conjure up strife. When we compare ourselves to Christ, however, we see that we all fall short of His glory, and we see that everyone needs grace. Even as He gives grace to us, we must impart grace to others. Paul warned against false comparison. (See 2 Corinthians 10:12.) Every family member is a unique child of God. Fathers, like the Father, are not to show favoritism. (See Acts 10:34.) They develop an atmosphere in the family of mutual love, respect, honor, and caring for one another.

Always Becoming

A godly father is constantly developing his family members to grow in God's limitless potential, to be their best through His strength, and to accept others as they are growing in Christ. He stretches his wife and children to achieve their utmost for His highest. He continually tests the character and abilities of his children. When assisting them with their homework, for example, he will not give them the answers but will help them learn how to solve the problems. When they are facing tough decisions, he will not always tell them what to do. He will teach them right from wrong and how to make godly decisions based on the nature and character of God.

The objective of development is permanent growth. The father cultivates his relationship with his wife and children so that they will grow beyond themselves and into the believers God purposed them to be. The powerful message of 2 Corinthians 5:17 is that new creations in Christ are continually having old things—sin, bad habits, ignorance, and strongholds—pass away, while all areas of life are becoming new. Fathers understand that God's children are always becoming! We are developing and growing into Christ's image. We are being changed *"from glory to glory"* (2 Corinthians 3:18 KJV). Fathers put a badge on their family members, including themselves, which reads, "Please be patient with me. God isn't finished with me yet!"

> **A father encourages his family members to grow in God's limitless potential.**

Fathers develop fathers. A man learns how to father from a father. A father grows in fatherhood by leaning on the heavenly Father. The goal of fathering is to develop men who can father and women who can mother under the covering of a godly husband. So when your son starts to make decisions as good as or better than you have been making, you can affirm to him that he is now a father while continuing to encourage him as a father.

Jesus promised that when we are in the Father and the Father is in us, just as the Father is in Him, then we will do greater works than He did. (See John 14:12.) The application for fatherhood is that a successful father will produce a child who is greater than himself.

CHAPTER PRINCIPLES

1. As developers, fathers plan, prepare, plant, protect, and produce that which God has placed in their care.

2. The godly father who develops his family has a plan for their orderly growth: physically, intellectually, emotionally, and spiritually.

3. A godly father is an example of holiness for his family and develops them to be the light of the world, the salt of the earth, and witnesses for Christ.

4. Development creates an environment that allows others to encounter learning experiences under the guidance of a father's wisdom.

5. The objective of development is permanent growth. A godly father provides encouragement, positive feedback, and an opportunity to try and fail, and he does not make comparisons.

6. A husband and father stretches his wife and children to achieve their utmost for God's highest. He cultivates his relationship with his family members so they can grow beyond themselves and be the believers God purposed them to be.

7. Fathers develop fathers. A man learns how to father from a father. A father grows in fatherhood by leaning on God the Father.

Part 3

═══════════════════════════

FULFILLING YOUR PURPOSE AS A FATHER

Chapter 11

UNDERSTANDING PURPOSE
AND ROLES

W e've explored ten functions of fathers and how males are the foundation and anchor of their families. In this chapter, I want to address the subject of fatherhood from an overall cultural perspective. This will enable you to better comprehend how to put into practice everything we've been discussing.

In my book *Understanding the Purpose and Power of Men,* I explain why many men are having difficulty determining what it means to be a real man (and consequently a true father) in our modern society. One of the things I deal with is the role factor. For centuries, in many cultures, the male has determined his manhood from the roles he's played in society. Men were considered men based on what they did more than on who they were. The societal roles were clear, and men knew what they were supposed to do in life. For example, as long as a husband could provide a house, food, clothing, and security for his wife and children, he was considered a man. The woman's job was to cook, clean, care for the children, and provide sex for the man. Once she did that, she was a woman.

These were mutually understood and mutually dependent roles. The wife depended on her husband completely to fulfill his role, and he depended on her completely to fulfill hers. In many cases, couples didn't think about love as much as helping one another survive. It was a partnership. That's one reason why most people up until contemporary times didn't get divorced.

> **The only way for a man to live out his fatherhood nature is to focus on his purpose.**

For several decades, however, we have been living in a transitional time, and these roles are not as clear as they used to be. Perhaps your father or grandfather told you, "Be a man." You asked, "What does it mean to be a man?" And he supplied the above definition: provide a house, food, clothing, and security. When you went out on your own, however, and ran into a pretty woman, you discovered a problem with this plan: she already had a car, owned her own home, bought her own food, carried mace for protection, didn't need your money, and perhaps didn't even care if you had any (and maybe already had children, as well).

The situation became even more complicated when she told you, "I'm looking for a real man." You said, "Okay, I'm going to marry you and buy you a house and provide you with food, clothes, and security." She said, "I have all that, but I want you to be a man."

Many women do not depend on men in the way they used to, and this is a crisis for many men. Males and females, even in the church, are experiencing stress because they often seem to be going in different directions. Men no longer know what it means to be a husband or what their identity as a man should be. The old formula isn't working anymore. A number of women make more money than the men, and the men are living off their wives' salaries. Maybe your grandfather said, "If she doesn't behave, put your foot down." You tell him, "It's her floor!" He said, "You let her know who is wearing the pants in the family!" You say, "She wears them, too!" Men and women often don't *complete* each other; they *compete* with each other in the home.

You Must Know Your Purpose

To make it through this crisis of social change and become true fathers, we must once more reconnect to God's concept of manhood in Genesis, which transcends culture and time because it is part of His plan in creation. The only way for a man to discover and live out his inherent fatherhood nature is to maintain a focus on purpose rather than roles that are related to a certain culture or time in history. Purpose is the key to manhood and fatherhood.

Again, Genesis 2:15 says, *"The LORD God took the man, and put him into the garden of Eden to dress it and to keep it"* (KJV). God *put* Adam in the garden of Eden. He didn't allow the man to wander around in an attempt to find it. He also did not leave Eden as an option, which means that Eden is a requirement for a male. God made the man and told him, "This is where you belong."

After placing him in Eden, God commanded the man to work: he was to cultivate the garden. Remember that work was given to the male even before the female was created. Note also that work came before the fall. Just to set the record straight, work is not a part of the curse! As I indicated earlier, we can cause it to be a curse for ourselves and our families if we make it an idol and become workaholics. But work itself is a gift from God. The man was also instructed to *"keep"* or care for the garden. In the Hebrew, this word donates guarding, watching over, preserving, and protecting it.[7]

Vital Purposes of the Male

Genesis 2:15 reveals five vital purposes of a male, which women need to be aware of also. But men need to know these purposes first to bring restoration to their own lives and to their families. As we have seen, most men were never taught these principles, and that's why they are having problems. These five purposes of the male involve doing, but they are not based on what a man does; rather, they are natural outcomes of who he is. We will use them as a brief summary of the fatherhood purposes we have explored throughout this book and as a reminder of the male's purpose, priority, and role on earth as he reflects the nature of God the Father.

To Dwell in God's Presence

The first thing God gave the male was Eden. The word *Eden* in Hebrew is written with five strokes, each stroke a symbol representing a word or a character. My study of the five strokes indicated *spot, moment, presence, open door,* and *delightful place.* Here is my interpretation of the word. God took the man and put him in a spot, for the moment, where the presence of God was an open door to heaven. In essence, Eden is not a place but an atmosphere.

---

[7] See *Strong's Exhaustive Concordance,* #H8104 and the *New American Standard Exhaustive Concordance of the Bible* (NASC), The Lockman Foundation, #H8104. Used by permission.

The Scripture says that the Lord *"planted"* (Genesis 2:8) or established, the garden. He established a spot on the earth where His presence literally came down from heaven and touched so that it was a door of open access to heaven. Adam didn't have to do anything "religious" to enter the presence of God. He had open access to Him. He walked and talked directly with God in the cool of the day.

Why did God give Eden to the male first, before He gave him the female? Because God knew what he was going to do with this man. Remember that in Adam's body was the initial seed for all humanity, and He would bring everybody into existence through him. He wanted the male to have access to Him so he could always know the will of God for those who came out of him. In other words, being in God's presence is essential for accessing the instruction you need to lead your family in God's ways.

In putting the man in Eden, therefore, the first thing God gave him was His own presence. Likewise, the first thing you need in your life—whether you are a policeman, a politician, a CEO, a mechanic, an IT specialist, a doctor, a carpenter, or anything else—is the presence of God. You need God's presence before you need the presence of a woman. As a matter of fact, Adam was already in Eden when God brought Eve and presented her to him. Eve met Adam in Eden. Where do you meet women?

For a male, the presence of God is like water to a fish, or soil to a plant. If you take the fish out of water, or the plant out of soil, it malfunctions and dies. If you take the male out of God's presence, he will malfunction and die. This is why Satan will do anything possible to keep a man like you away from the presence of God, which is attracted by your worship. As we saw earlier, the devil doesn't care so much if women enter God's presence because they are not the foundation. But Satan makes sure the men drop the women off at church and then go to play or watch sports or do some other activity. Professional sports matches are broadcast all day on Sunday, tempting men to stay home rather than be in God's presence. When they do go to church, many men feel ashamed to lift their hands to the God who made them; Satan doesn't want you ever to feel comfortable worshiping God, because when you worship God, you attract His presence.

> Work is not something you do; it is something you become—to manifest what God put inside you.

When a man gets into God's presence, when he falls in love with God's presence, that man begins to function. The Bible says that God dwells in the praises of His people. (See Psalm 22:3 KJV.) In Israel, the priests were the ones who led the worship—and all the priests were men. But today, when you bring a man into a worship service, he sits there as cool as a cucumber. He's too cool to say amen, too cool to clap, too cool to lift his hands, too cool to sing to God. He doesn't realize Satan has him cold, because he doesn't want him to get into God's presence. At home, many men make their wives lead family devotions. The devil doesn't want you to start leading devotions because the presence of God will come to your house if you do. When my children were growing up, every morning I would say to them, "We are going to sing praises to God."

Do you think you're too tough to worship? Who wrote the book in the Bible that's filled with worship and praise? It was someone who killed a lion and a bear with his bare hands. He killed a ten-foot giant with a rock. Anyone can sit down in a pew and fold his arms. It takes a giant-slayer like David to write things like, *"O Lord, our Lord, how majestic is your name in all the earth! You have set your glory above the heavens"* (Psalm 8:1), and *"I will extol the Lord at all times; his praise will always be on my lips. My soul will boast in the Lord"* (Psalm 34:1–2). I love to worship more than anything else. I've led worship in our church for years. I've written books on it. Worship is the most important thing in my life because it protects the rest of my life. Psalm 150:6 says, *"Let everything that has breath praise the Lord."*

When you become ashamed of public worship, you are an embarrassment to God's assignment for you as a man. On Sunday, you should be the first one at church, sitting up front, because you are the worship leader, not your wife, sisters, or daughters. The first thing that makes you a man is your capacity to enter Eden.

To Manifest What God Put inside You

The second purpose of a male is work, which actually means to manifest what God put inside you. I researched this word and found that in one sense *work* means "to become." Work is not something you do; it is something you become. What are you becoming?

The reason many people are poor and struggling is that they have found a job but have never found their true work. A job is not designed to prosper you. It is designed to pay bills. A man is someone who has discovered who and what he is supposed to become. You are alive because there's some work God wanted manifested on earth that He buried inside you.

He wants you to reveal it. You are not a mistake. When you "go to work," you are actually to "go to become."

When you go to your job every day, are you becoming what you dreamed of? Perhaps you are in the right place with your employment and you thank God for it. But too many people's jobs stop them from becoming. They are told what to do, when to do it, how long to do it, and when to go home. There's no room for them to become, and their manhood is stifled by a job they hate. Every Monday morning, they're depressed as they sit in traffic on their way to their jobs because it is not their true work.

> While purpose is why you were born, vision is when you start seeing it yourself.

Work reveals the potential God has placed within you. Suppose I have a mango seed, and I plant it and say to it, "Work." I'm telling it that I want to see a tree with mangos that have their own seed in them and can nourish people. I'm telling it, "I know that inside of you there is a potential you must reveal: a mango tree." Work, to a mango seed, is becoming a mango tree with mangos that provide nutrients for the community. Notice what happens when the mango tree fulfills its purpose. No mango tree eats its own mangos. They are not for their own benefit but for the benefit of people. They bring people health.

You, too, were born with something "trapped" in you that the world is supposed to benefit from, and that's your work. Many men are afraid to talk about their dreams, but God is saying to you, "Manifest yourself! I want to see what I put into you."

I don't have a "job" anymore, but I used to. I worked for the Bahamas government for twelve years. I taught junior high school for five years. I worked in a food store before that, packing shelves. I worked in a warehouse lifting boxes. I worked in an ad firm, doing advertisments, drawings, and so forth. These were learning experiences. But then I found my true work of helping others understand how to manifest their God-given leadership potential. I don't wake up in the morning and "go" to work. I wake up and become what God created me to be.

Jesus said, *"Let your light so shine before men, that they may see your good works, and glorify your Father which is in heaven"* (Matthew 5:16 KJV). When other people see your work, when they see you manifesting what God put into you, they will glorify God. You were born to do something so awesome that only God could get the credit for it. Some of the most remarkable people in the world are reading this book, and the world doesn't know it yet. Your work is your purpose, and your purpose is the original intent of your Creator. Purpose is the reason you were born; it's why you exist.

While purpose is why you were born, vision is when you start seeing it yourself. I believe most men have already been seeing or sensing their purpose, but it is so big that they're afraid of it. Their dreams frighten them. That's why they settle for jobs they hate. Let me tell you something about God's vision and work in your life: if God's assignment for you *doesn't* frighten you, I question whether it's really His purpose. A God-given purpose can only be fulfilled through His guidance and strength.

What Is Vision?

- Vision is purpose in pictures.

- Vision is the capacity to see beyond your physical eyes. A male should never live only by what he sees.

- Vision is "finished purpose." That's why you can see it.

- Vision is your future, but since God has already planned it, it's in His "past." Whatever you were born to do is already finished in Him. *"Many are the plans in a man's heart, but it is the Lord's purpose that prevails"* (Proverbs 19:21). God's purpose for your life as a male is already established; He's not worried about your future. He wants you to cease worrying about it and start making plans to go there.

Have you been seeing pictures of your dream? When you turn the TV and computer off, and everything is quiet, do you start thinking of your future? Your dreams are close to you, but they're being drowned out by your music, your phone, and other people talking. In the Bible, whenever God wanted to speak to a man about his work, He always took him away from other people. God took Abraham to a mountain all by himself. He took Moses to the desert. David heard from God when he was out tending sheep in the hills. You can't hear God's plan if you are always around other people, always in the midst of a group of friends. God needs to isolate you so you can see pictures of your future again.

Purpose produces vision, and a vision produces a plan. Once there's a plan, it produces discipline in you. Write down your purpose, and then get some pictures symbolizing that purpose and what you need to fulfill it, and put them on your refrigerator. I cut out pictures of my dream and put them where I could see them every day. And I would say, "That's what I'm going to do." I remember the first day I put a picture of an airplane on my refrigerator. I needed one because of the numerous speaking engagements I have. My son asked, "Dad, what are you doing?" I said, "I'm looking at my future." I also remember my first flight in that aircraft with my son. He said, "Daddy, it came off the refrigerator!" I said, "Yes, Son, you have to see it first!"

Stop thinking small. Your dreams are not crazy. They are your work. Staying in a job that is not right for you is like a fish trying to be a horse. That's why you have high blood pressure. That's why there's so much stress in your life. You're doing things you weren't born to do.

A woman was created by God to help a man, but the man has to be doing something! God's purpose for creating the female was to help the male with his purpose-assignment. That's how important your purpose is. If you don't know what you were born to do, don't get married yet. If you are already married, and you don't know your purpose, your wife is probably living with frustration. When a man finds his work, a woman finds her assignment. I believe many marriages are breaking up because women are not helping their husbands with the work God has given them. Your wife is waiting for you to find your purpose because her assignment in life is tied to it. She was designed to help you. She may also have her own work, but for her to help you fulfill yours, you have to know your purpose.

God designed everything with the ability to fulfill its purpose. He designed a female to help a male, so everything God put in the female works toward that purpose. That's why a woman is such a frightening creature. She is one mean helping machine. When she shows up in your life, she has everything you need. She has insight, intuition, stamina, wisdom, counsel, the ability to carry burdens, and the capacity to incubate ideas. She can talk about your vision and protect your resources. She comes with a keen mind, academic degrees, and psychological stability. Some men call all this "aggression." Do you know why they call it that? Women come to them with excellent qualities and resources to help them, but they aren't doing anything, and so they are intimidated. And then this is what happens: since the men aren't doing anything for them to help with, the women don't want to waste what they have, so they help themselves. They start their own businesses with the gifts they would have used to help their husbands. Now the husbands get even more jealous and angry. So it's vital for men to understand their purpose in life.

> You must be anchored to your God-given purpose in order to give your family direction in difficult times.

How can you know what your purpose is? I want you to make a commitment to discover and pursue your work. Ask God to reveal it to you as you seek. He says, *"I am God, and there is none like me. I make known the end from the beginning, from ancient times, what is still to come. I say: My purpose will stand, and I will do all that I please"* (Isaiah 46:9–10). You were not born just to make a living, but you were born to start something that is already finished in the mind of God. That is why you dream. Make a commitment to the purpose of God for your life, and to the God of that purpose.

In chapter two, we talked about the male as the anchor of the family. You must be anchored to your God-given purpose in order to give your family direction in difficult times. Even though the storm rages, the billows come over your head, and the winds blow and break the mast, if your anchor is already attached to your purpose, you will arrive safely at your destination. To be tough in tough times, you have to know where you're going.

Here are some practical keys to helping you find your purpose in life, drawn from my book *The Principles and Power of Vision*. Ask yourself:

- *What is my deepest desire?*
- *What is my reoccurring dream—the one that doesn't go away?*
- *What do I desire to change in the world?* Many men have thoughts of this nature every day, but they drown them out. There's something in your mind and heart that bothers you, and you say to yourself, "I wish I could change that in the world." Whatever that thing is, it may be what you were born to do.
- *What makes me angry?* Whenever you see what you were born to change, it makes you angry. If you hate corruption in government, you may be called to be a public servant or a reporter. If you hate to see young people hanging around in the street with nothing to do, you were probably meant to work with young people and solve their problems. If you hate sickness with a passion, you may have been born to be a medical practitioner. Think about whatever makes you angry and what you might do to change it.
- *What is my deepest passion?* You have to find out what you could do for the rest of your life even if you were never paid for it. The amazing thing is that, when you find it, you will get paid for it because you will exhibit the energy,

commitment, knowledge, and skills that cause people to notice you.

- *What am I willing to die for?* Perhaps you have never thought about this question before. That's why your life has little depth and meaning. I would die for what I do. I was born to raise up Third World leaders and to train Third World people to think like leaders. My mission statement is "Transforming followers into leaders and leaders into agents of change." That's my life in one sentence. You have to be able to articulate your purpose in one sentence. Jesus said, *"The Son of Man did not come to be served, but to…give his life as a ransom for many"* (Matthew 20:28). Essentially, He was saying, "I'm a ransom." That was His mission in one sentence. He didn't say, "I am going to give you ransom," but "I have come to give *My life* as a ransom." Remember that your work is what you are. Jesus is a ransom. I am a leader-trainer. *What are you?*

Start dreaming. Close your eyes and see the future. Perhaps you are thinking, "I wish I had known this twenty years ago. I would be much farther along in life than I am now." It's not too late. Say, "I'm starting today. I'm going from my job toward my work." Let God speak to you about His purpose for you.

You don't want to waste another day on just a job. You don't want to waste the next ten years struggling with what it means to be a man who fulfills his purpose. Let God show you again the dream you threw away. Ask God to shine on you the same light He shone on Moses so you can see and hear your purpose. Ask Him to show you what makes you angry, the thing that won't leave you, the passion in your heart. None of us knows everything, regardless of our education, knowledge, and experience. We need God to direct us in our purpose and vision. As an act of obedience, go before God and say, "Connect me to my purpose; anchor me to my destiny. I commit to reading Your Word so that I can know Your commands. I break my ego. I bow my pride before You. Show me who I am. Give me a desire for Eden. Help me to want to be in Your presence. Without You, I can do nothing. I surrender to the lordship of Jesus. He knows what's inside me—the 'seed' of my life. Let me hear His voice; speak to Me again. Reveal Yourself to me. I've gone about things in my own way. I've tried my own things.

> You are designed to bring out the best in everything under your care.

I've made my own plans. But I come to You now and say, 'Your kingdom come, Your will be done. Not my will, but Yours, be done.'"

To Be a Cultivator

The third purpose of the man is to be a cultivator. We talked about the father's function of cultivation earlier, but I want you to fully realize that you do not just cultivate—you are by nature a cultivator. You are a cultivator designed by God. This means you are one who improves things, who maximizes the potential of the people and resources around you. You are designed to bring out the best in everything under your care. This is why God will not give you a finished product. For example, He won't give you a business. Instead, He'll give you an idea and say, "I want you to bring the best out of that. Cultivate it." I built my organization from seven people to one hundred full-time workers with the potential of reaching millions of people every week. People see the organization for what it is today, but I had to cultivate it every single day of the last thirty years.

Men are cultivators. God hid products and resources in the physical world and watched to see what we would do with them. Did you know that 98 percent of all inventions are by males? You will never be given a finished product by God. He'll only give you raw material. God won't even give you a completed woman. The perfect woman you are looking for does not exist. Many men get divorced because they are disappointed in the women they married. They don't understand that you have to cultivate your wife. God will give you a woman who is "raw material." It is your job to love her as God loves her by helping her maximize her potential, improve her life situation, and be the best she can be.

> Men are designed by God to be cultivators who don't just sit on good ideas but implement them.

When I first married my wife, she was so introverted that I had to make her talk to me. Four people were too much of a crowd for her. She was afraid of expressing herself. When I discovered being a cultivator was part of my purpose as a husband (father), I began to draw out of her what she really had inside her. Today, my wife travels around the world ministering and speaking to thousands and tens of thousands of people. This is the woman who was afraid to be in a room with four people. God wants you to help your wife fulfill the plans He has for her.

The Scripture says,

Husbands, love your wives, just as Christ loved the church and gave himself up for her to make her holy, cleansing her by the washing with water through the word, and to present her to himself as a radiant church, without stain or wrinkle or any other blemish, but holy and blameless.

(Ephesians 6:26–27)

Jesus Christ is a Husband. His wife's name is *Ecclesia* (the church, the bride of Christ). He will minister to her and develop her until she is "radiant" and everything He desires her to be. He will present her as a glorious bride. This is the way husbands are to love their wives. In other words, if you are not proud of your wife, you are the failure. If you are ashamed of your wife, you should be ashamed of yourself. The more you criticize her, the more evidence there is of your failure. Instead, the longer your wife lives with you, the better she should become. A good man brings out the best in his wife.

Men, therefore, are designed by God to be cultivators who don't just sit on good ideas but implement them, who don't complain about others but see their potential and help them reach it. Ask God to start working out the ideas He has put within you. Tell Him you are sorry for your procrastination, and decide today that you will begin to cultivate them. Repent for criticizing your wife and children, discover their hidden potential, and lovingly cultivate what God has placed within them.

To Be a Protector

The fourth purpose of the male is to protect. Even though many women may feel they are able to protect themselves, you are still called to be the protector of your family. Remember that God told Adam to guard everything in the garden. You were designed to guard and defend, and to cover everything under your care and in your sphere of influence. That includes your wife, your children, your neighbors, and your community.

> **Men are called to protect their families and communities from the destructive currents of our modern society.**

Many men don't think about protecting others—they think about how they can use them. As I wrote earlier, if you are a single man on a date with a young lady, you are supposed to protect her from even your own sexual desires. She is supposed to feel safe in your automobile. You are supposed to guard her virginity, not destroy it. Real men protect; they don't seduce. Again, God designed you with physical strength in order to defend women, not to use your strength to overpower them. That is abuse of power. You are supposed to be the safest place any woman can be.

How many men use their gifts to destroy women? Christ protected women! He was a guard for them. Children were safe with Him. He didn't abuse them. He blessed them. A good man always leaves a woman better when she leaves his presence. Let this be the last day you misuse a woman. Say, "Lord, forgive me for any time that I have used, manipulated, or abused a woman. Forgive me, and may they forgive me. Today, I am a guard, a protector, and a preserver. Amen."

Men are called to protect their families and communities from the negative and destructive currents of our modern society. Remember our definition of an anchor? It is "a reliable or principal support: mainstay," "something that serves to hold an object firmly," and "anything that gives stability and security."

If a boat is drifting with a current, and you put the anchor down on a rock, it stops the boat from being controlled by the current. This is very important for males. The current of our modern society is filled with so many strong influences to do all kinds of unhealthy things that the male needs to come back in the family, put his anchor on the rock of a solid principle, and say, "We're not going in that direction."

Note that an anchor does not stop the current; the current will come. Rather, it stops the boat you are in. How many things have you stopped from happening to your son? How many things have you stopped from happening to your daughter? You see your daughter wearing certain clothes or looking a certain way, or you see your son watching something inappropriate on the Internet, and you say, "No, not in this house." A male is an anchor, and an anchor stops things. You know that your daughter and son are being taught in school that homosexuality and lesbianism are acceptable, and they're coming home and beginning to talk to you about whether it is right or wrong, and you as a kingdom father have to put the anchor down and stop them and say, "That's not for us." Many times, I had to tell my son and daughter, "That music—not in this house. That type of clothing—not in this house. This boat is anchored." And they made it through

> We need men who know the Word, not men who know the names of every player on their favorite basketball team.

the turbulent waves. They are upstanding young people who don't have memories they can't enjoy.

An anchor stops things. As a pastor, you are supposed to be the anchor of your church. When divisive things are happening in your church, and you know they're happening, you have to put your foot down like an anchor and say, "Not in this ministry." You're the foundation. Men, in whatever setting you're in—home, church, school, work, or community— you are designed to protect those around you—the weak, the vulnerable, the oppressed, women, children, your brothers. A real man is a protecting man.

To Be a Teacher

Fifth, the male's purpose is to teach the instructions God gave him. As I wrote earlier, you need to learn the Word of God so you can be in a position to become the one who teaches. Whatever God calls for, He provides for. Whatever God creates something to do, He builds in the capacity to do it. God built you with the teacher psyche. Men in all countries are wired to be teachers. The problem is that many of them don't know the lessons.

You are the teacher in your home. You are the one who is supposed to have the information, the instruction. It starts with you. That means you have to hear from God first. Perhaps you have never read the Bible. You may have read a few verses from Psalms, but you've never read the Bible from Genesis to Revelation. You're forty years old and you've never read the Bible, but you're attempting to be the head of the home!

Can you teach your wife the Word of God? Do you know enough of the Word to become the teacher of your children?

If the answer is no, get busy and make a commitment to read the New Testament first. We need men who know the Word, not men who know the football scores and the names of every player on their favorite basketball team. You know who got drafted, but you don't know who Malachi is or why his book in the Bible is important.

Realize you were born to be a teacher. That's why you hate it when you're driving and you're trying to find a certain place and your wife's saying, "I think we should turn here," and you say, "Be quiet; I'm driving." She says, "I think we just passed the road," and you say, "I'm driving." Yes, men, we're driving. After about twenty hours, we finally turn around and say, "You know, I think I might have missed it somewhere." And then we add, "Don't you dare say 'I told you so.'" Even when we're stupid, we don't want to be taught. When a man doesn't know, he doesn't want you to tell him he doesn't know. He wants to be a sophisticated fool.

I challenge you to read and study. I read four books a month because I am the foundation and anchor of my home. In a sense, I have two "houses": my home and my church. I have a house with two thousand people in it every week. When I'm on television, my house has 1.8 million people in it. I have a big house; I have to read even more because they listen to my instruction and I have to know what I am saying.

The Marks of a Man of Purpose

To sum up, here are the marks of a man of purpose:

- He loves Eden. He *loves* God's presence. He possesses a true self-image based on his knowledge that God created him in His own image. He knows who he is.

- He desires to work. If you meet a man who doesn't like work, he's not a real man, a man of purpose.
- He is able to cultivate.
- He commits to protect everything under his care.
- He knows the Word of God, and he teaches it.

What a beautiful picture of what a real man is—and what a picture of fatherhood that reflects Father God. If I were a woman, I'd marry that man right away. He knows who he is, where he is, and what he's supposed to be doing. He's able to cultivate, protect, and teach God's Word. That's the kind of man every woman is looking for. Many women are confused today because they can't find that man. They meet men who have high-paying jobs, wear nice clothes, and own expensive houses and cars, but who don't know what really matters. They meet men who are wandering aimlessly in life and unable to support themselves because they have no clear purpose. The women are asking, "What's happening?"

> You will discover your true image and purpose only in your Creator.

I want to see you change things in your life, family, job, ministry, and community by understanding and fulfilling your God-given purpose. You will discover your true image and purpose only in your Creator.

We now turn to our final issue in *The Fatherhood Principle*—fathering the fatherless.

CHAPTER PRINCIPLES

1. The only way for a man to discover and live out his inherent fatherhood nature in a time of social change is to maintain a focus on his God-given purpose rather than roles that are related to a certain culture or time in history.

2. Five vital purposes of the male are (1) to dwell in God's presence, (2) to manifest what God put inside you, (3) to be a cultivator, (4) to be a protector, and (5) to be a teacher.

3. When a man gets into God's presence, he begins to function again.

4. Work reveals the potential God has placed within you. You were born with something "trapped" in you that the world is supposed to benefit from.

5. God doesn't give males the finished product but the raw material with which to cultivate.

6. Men are designed to guard, defend, and cover everything under their care and in their spheres of influence.

7. The male must know God's Word in order to teach the instructions God gave him.

Chapter 12

FATHERING THE
FATHERLESS

I pray that fathers who read this book will receive the Spirit of the Father—not just for their own families, but also for the church and our culture. The spirit of a father is the awareness that everyone around a father is his responsibility.

As we have studied in Genesis, the woman and the family came out of the man. So every woman and child that a father meets is his responsibility if they are fatherless. Godly fathers must become fathers of their communities and nations. There are many women who have husbands who are not functioning in their lives as source and sustainer. There are many children who have only a biological father, not a true father. So we, as Christian fathers, must be sure that we take responsibility by praying for these families and supporting them in other ways so that they may be restored to their heavenly Father's plan for their lives.

There are also women and children who have lost husbands and fathers to divorce or death. James wrote, *"Religion that God our Father accepts as pure and faultless is this: to look after orphans and widows in their distress and to keep oneself from being polluted by the world"* (James 1:27). The fatherless should be fathered by Christian men who can step in the gap, sustaining and cultivating them.

David declared, *"A father to the fatherless, a defender of widows, is God in his holy dwelling. God sets the lonely in families"* (Psalm 68:5–6). What is the family into which God places the fatherless? It is His family, the church. We are to go wherever the fatherless are found and become a father and family to them. If you are a widow or a divorced woman, I encourage you to find a church that preaches the Word of God and has godly men and women who can strengthen you and your children in God's ways and who will be a family to you.

There's a fathering parable in Matthew 25 in which Jesus reveals that those who truly follow Him will father those who are in prison, hungry, naked, thirsty, sick, and strangers. Men, inasmuch as we father the least of these, we minister unto the Lord Himself.

Many of those in prison are men who never had a father like the Father. How do we heal that? Godly fathers must go out and father them. Recall once more the prophecy for our day in Malachi 4:6: *"He will turn the hearts of the fathers to their children, and the hearts of the children to their fathers; or else I* [God] *will come and strike the land with a curse."* When godly fathers fail to father the fatherless in a society, a curse comes upon that land. Scripture never mentions returning the hearts of the children back to the mothers because our greatest problem is a father problem.

We must incorporate the scriptural functions of fatherhood into our lives so that we will finally understand and fulfill our true priority, position, and role as males. God the Father is our Source. Masses of men must return to God the Father so that the children's hearts may be turned to their fathers and to God. We need men of the Spirit to be responsible as progenitors and providers for the future generations, and men who are fathers to be willing to sustain their offspring.

My friend Jesse Duplantis told me a story about when he was waiting at a traffic light in Louisiana and a man came up to his car. This man looked terrible, was wearing dirty clothes, and was carrying a piece of cardboard that said HELP THE POOR. The Holy Spirit spoke to Jesse and said, *Why do you think this man is poor?* He answered, *Maybe he can't find a job, maybe he has physical problems.* The Holy Spirit said, *No. This man is on the street today begging because of bad family relationships.* When he told me that story, my life was changed. I am from a family of eleven children, and my father is now in his eighties. I decided that none of my family would ever beg as long as I am alive. In other words, as long as there's a man in the house, no one will be on the street.

> The family in which God places the fatherless is His family— the church.

As a father—like *the* Father—remember that every child you meet is your responsibility. You are to support and pray for that child's father, or to be a father to the child if he or she is fatherless. Every woman you meet is your responsibility; she is to be treated with dignity and respect. Every elderly person you meet is your responsibility; he or she is to be treated as you would treat your own parent.

This book is a clarion call to men to be the fathers God the Father created them to be. It is time that fathers answer God's call to be responsible for the fatherless in their churches, communities, and nations. If the male doesn't hold like an anchor, society goes adrift and crashes on the rocks of immorality and broken values, and we lose the vision and destiny of the country and the programs and resources of the community. Everything falls apart when the anchor isn't holding.

In Africa, there is a well-known concept that has become familiar to many of us: "It takes a village to raise a child." That concept is also found in the Bible:

> *Just as each of us has one body with many members, and these members do not all have the same function, so in Christ we who are many form one body, and each member belongs to all the others.* (Romans 12:4–5)

> [An expert in the law] *wanted to justify himself, so he asked Jesus, "And who is my neighbor?" In reply Jesus said: "A man was going down from Jerusalem to Jericho, when he fell into the hands of robbers. They stripped him of his clothes, beat him and went away, leaving him half dead. A priest happened to be going down the same road, and when he saw the man, he passed by on the other side. So too, a Levite, when he came to the place and saw him, passed by on the other side. But a Samaritan, as he traveled, came where the man was; and when he saw him, he took pity on him. He went to him and bandaged his wounds, pouring on oil and wine. Then he put the man on his own donkey, took him to an inn and took care of him. The next day he took out two silver coins and gave them to the innkeeper. 'Look after him,' he said, 'and when I return, I will reimburse you for*

any extra expense you may have.' Which of these three do you think was a neighbor to the man who fell into the hands of robbers?" The expert in the law replied, "The one who had mercy on him." Jesus told him, "Go and do likewise."
(Luke 10:29–37)

The whole community is responsible for each person, and the destiny of each person is shaped by the whole community. We have a corporate responsibility to father our fatherless. We are not in this alone. Together, we are a community of faith; we are the church, which is God's family, in which every member supports and cares for every other member.

I believe that the church should form the most magnificent and magnanimous "adoption agency" in the twenty-first century. The way you change a nation is not by attacking the government, but by being a true father to your children and those who are fatherless. That's the way God did it in every situation. Godly fatherhood is the key to this generation and all to come.

> **Godly fatherhood is the key to this generation and all to come.**

Consider this final thought: God's Son entered into this world and had to be adopted by an earthly father—Joseph. Joseph could have rejected Mary as supposedly having been unfaithful to him and gotten pregnant by another man, but he didn't. He believed what God told him through the angel. At great personal risk and sacrifice to himself, Joseph stepped out responsibly and became the earthly father of Jesus, Savior of the world.

Fathers, be like the heavenly Father to your own families, communities, and nations. Ask Him to fill up any empty spots in your life that your father couldn't fill. Forgive your father if he wasn't there for you, or if he was alcoholic or abusive. Go to your heavenly Father, and let Him make you a strong foundation, a secure anchor, so you can help bring healing to the land, restoring individuals and families. Then future generations will rise up and give glory to our Father.

CHAPTER PRINCIPLES

1. The spirit of a father is the awareness that everyone around a father is his responsibility.

2. Godly fathers become fathers of their communities and nations.

3. As Christian fathers, we are to go to wherever the fatherless are found and become fathers and families to them.

4. When we incorporate the fatherhood functions in our lives, we will finally understand our true priority, position, and role as males.

5. By being a father like God the Father to your family, community, and nation, you will help bring healing to the land, and future generations will rise up and give glory to our heavenly Father.

ABOUT THE AUTHOR

D r. Myles Munroe is an international motivational speaker, best-selling author, educator, leadership mentor, and consultant for government and business. Traveling extensively throughout the world, Dr. Munroe addresses critical issues affecting the full range of human, social, and spiritual development. The central theme of his message is the maximization of individual potential, including the transformation of followers into leaders and leaders into agents of change.

Dr. Munroe is founder and president of Bahamas Faith Ministries International (BFMI), a multidimensional organization headquartered in Nassau, Bahamas. He is chief executive officer and chairman of the board of the International Third World Leaders Association and president of the International Leadership Training Institute.

Dr. Munroe is also the founder and executive producer of a number of radio and television programs aired worldwide. In addition, he is a frequent guest on other television and radio programs and international networks and is a contributing writer for various Bible editions, journals, magazines, and newsletters, such as *The Believer's Topical Bible, The African Cultural Heritage Topical Bible, Charisma Life Christian Magazine,* and *Ministries Today.* A popular author of over forty books, his works include *The Most Important Person on Earth, The Spirit of*

Leadership, The Principles and Power of Vision, Understanding the Purpose and Power of Prayer, Understanding the Purpose and Power of Woman, and *Understanding the Purpose and Power of Men.*

Dr. Munroe has changed the lives of multitudes around the world with a powerful message that inspires, motivates, challenges, and empowers people to discover personal purpose, develop true potential, and manifest their unique leadership abilities. For over thirty years, he has trained tens of thousands of leaders in business, industry, education, government, and religion. He personally addresses over 500,000 people each year on personal and professional development. His appeal and message transcend age, race, culture, creed, and economic background.

Dr. Munroe has earned B.A. and M.A. degrees from Oral Roberts University and the University of Tulsa, and he has been awarded a number of honorary doctoral degrees. He has also served as an adjunct professor of the Graduate School of Theology at Oral Roberts University.

Dr. Munroe and his wife Ruth travel as a team and are involved in teaching seminars together. Both are leaders who minister with sensitive hearts and international vision. They are the proud parents of two college graduates, Charisa and Chairo (Myles, Jr.).

THE ISLANDS OF THE
bahamas

For Information on Religious Tourism
Email: ljohnson@bahamas.com

1.800.224.3681

www.worship.bahamas.com

The Principles and Power of Vision
Dr. Myles Munroe

Whether you are a businessperson, a student, a homemaker, or a head of state, best-selling author Dr. Myles Munroe explains how you can make your dreams and hopes a living reality. Your success is not dependent on the state of the economy or what the job market is like. You do not need to be hindered by the limited perceptions of others or by a lack of resources. Discover time-tested principles that will enable you to fulfill your vision no matter who you are or where you come from.

Revive your passion for living, pursue your dream, discover your vision—and find your true life.

ISBN: 978-0-88368-951-6 • Hardcover • 240 pages

The Spirit of Leadership
Dr. Myles Munroe

After personally training thousands of leaders from around the world, best-selling author Dr. Myles Munroe reports that while all people possess leadership potential, many do not understand how to cultivate the leadership nature and how to apply it to their lives. Discover the unique attitudes that all effective leaders exhibit, how to eliminate hindrances to your leadership abilities, and how to fulfill your particular calling in life. With wisdom and power, Dr. Munroe reveals a wealth of practical insights that will move you from being a follower to becoming the leader you were meant to be!

ISBN: 978-0-88368-983-7 • Hardcover • 304 pages

WHITAKER
HOUSE

www.whitakerhouse.com